9/23

$2—

A TALLY OF TYPES

A

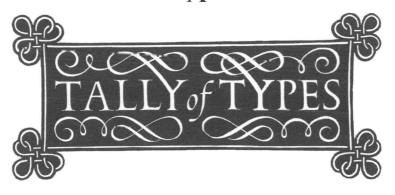

BY
STANLEY MORISON

WITH ADDITIONS
BY SEVERAL HANDS

AND WITH A NEW
INTRODUCTION BY
MIKE PARKER

DAVID R. GODINE, PUBLISHER
BOSTON

First published in 1999 by
DAVID R. GODINE, PUBLISHER, INC.
BOX 450
Jaffrey, New Hampshire 03452

Originally printed in a private edition in 1953.
A new edition, with revisions, was published in 1973.

"Monotype" is a registered trademark.

Library of Congress Cataloging in Publication Data
Morison, Stanley, 1889-1967.
A tally of types : with additions by several hands /
edited by Brooke Crutchley.
p.   cm.
Includes index.
ISBN 1-56792-004-7
1. Type and type-founding—Great Britain—History—20th century.
2. Monotype Corporation—History—20th century.
3. Morison, Stanley, 1889-1967. 4. Cambridge University Press—
History—20th century. 5. University presses—England—
Cambridge—History—20th century.
I. Crutchley, Brooke. II. Title.
Z250.A2M856 1995   95-35330
686.2'24—DC20   CIP

First printing, 1999
This book was printed on acid-free paper.
Printed in the United States of America

CONTENTS

PREFACE
TO THE
NEW EDITION

A Tally of Types first appeared in 1953, privately printed by the Cambridge University Printer, Brooke Crutchley, for presentation at Christmas to friends in printing and publishing.

In 1973 a trade edition was published by the Cambridge University Press; it differed from the original in a number of features, but Morison's account of the Monotype faces introduced at Cambridge between 1922 and 1932 remained unchanged, as it does in the present edition. It was supplemented by the appendix and notes which appear on pp. 111–133.

This, the third edition, has an introduction by Mike Parker, who followed Harry Carter to the Plantin Moretus Museum in Antwerp in 1957, where he took two years to organize the collection of 16th century punches, matrices for a seminal publication on the Museum's typographic holdings. At Mergenthaler Linotype he directed an expansion of the firm's hot metal library while anticipating and mastering the requirements of the future digital image-setting world. He is known as a principal founder of Bitstream, one of the first digital type foundries, The Company, and Pages Software, an experimental software program that allows writers and editors options for modular page design. He has thus come full circle, completing a process that began with Gutenberg's transformation of flexible but laborious calligraphy into modular fonts of movable type and ends with similar digital modules of expert design that guide all aspects of a document's appearance.

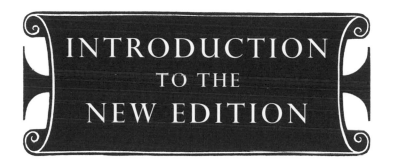

INTRODUCTION TO THE NEW EDITION

This slender book entered my life quietly enough in the spring of 1956 as I was completing my master's thesis on Garamont's types at Yale. At Alvin Eisenman's suggestion, I examined his copy of the original Cambridge Christmas book. A year's work was obsolete. Morison's passages on Garamont described him and his work with startling new clarity and authority, but without footnotes giving sources. My letter to Morison was promptly answered, revealing that the new information originated with Harry Carter's reconnaissance of the typographical material surviving at the Plantin-Moretus Museum in Antwerp, Belgium. The young curators, Leon Voet and H. D. L. Vervliet, were opening the definitive resources of the museum to international scholars. Morison's letter led me back to Alvin, then to Ray Nash at Dartmouth, his mentor and pioneer in the formulation and teaching of American typography, who helped me to obtain a grant from the Belgian American Educational Foundation, which took me to Antwerp and the Museum. The work led me to Harry, Ella and Matthew Carter at Oxford, to Netty Hoeflake at Enschedé, to Ellic Howe, John and Irène Dreyfus, Stanley Morison and Beatrice Warde in London, and finally, three eventful years later, to Jackson Burke at Mergenthaler Linotype in Brooklyn, New York, the start of a life in type.

The *Tally* provides more than the historical information that excited me. It casts a strong if sometimes oblique light on every part of the design and industrial creation of typefaces, on Morison's use of historical models and links to designers, on the relationship of type design to publishing, and on the organisation of the companies that manufactured type. It tells of the creation of a group of type-faces that lie at the heart of the library of book faces we all use today in our new world of digital communication.

To appreciate the brilliance of the Monotype achievement, one must understand something of the situations that lie all but unmentioned beneath Morison's account. Linotype and Monotype entered a world where one could choose types from any of hundreds of foundries, and combine them to typeset any manuscript. With the age of composing machines, each letter became an intricate machine-part, the matrix. Your only source of matrices was the manufacturer of your equipment.

Manufacturing executives faced two immense and immediate problems: first, to craft letters of apparently handset quality to run on intricate and obdurate machines, and then to choose or create a grand library of designs that would enable the equipment to assume its place in the world.

Those who planned to reshape any type, old or new, for use on a mechanical composing machine required the ultimate in craft and craftsmen if the effects of deforming mechanical requirements were not to be apparent on the page.

In 1899 the Monotype Corporation of London engaged Frank Hinman Pierpont as Works Manager to build and run the Mono-type factories at Salfords, in Surrey. Pierpont was a Connecticut engineer, a brilliant autocrat with a passion for quality in equipment, and a feeling for spacing and shape in type. He came to Monotype from Berlin, where he had been the managing director of the Typograph Aktiengesellschaft, a company that briefly competed with Linotype. Although Typograph is remembered today for the manually operated display device that survived at Ludlow, the original Typograph was a complex keyboard driven linecaster invented by John R. Rogers in 1890.

As Works Manager, Pierpont's inflexible pursuit of disciplined accuracy has become Monotype legend. He brought to Salfords his own team, headed by Fritz Max Stelzer. He had Stelzer manage the letterdrawing office, although his own passion for the craft led him to oversee in detail the preparation of each new typeface. He built a major library of typefaces suited to British taste and manufactured the matrices to British standards.

For the first twenty-five years Pierpont's matrices ran on keyboards and casters designed and built in America. Production of munitions 1914–1918 expanded Pierpont's factories and led management to move beyond peripherals. In 1924, shortly after Morison became Monotype's typographical adviser, a wholly British line of equipment began to appear from Salfords. At his death in 1937 Pierpont had sixty-nine refinements to machine tools and typesetting machines patented in his name, attesting to his engineering abilities and hinting at the originality of thought behind the autocracy. [1]

Pierpont was trained in preparing typefaces for linecasting machines, an operation demanding tight discipline if good character shape and spacing was to be achieved. The system allowed no kerning, and in its fully developed form required each character in italic and boldface fonts to adopt the width of the roman letter. The early Monotype systems in particular were similarly Procrustean and required equal discipline. The Monotype diecase contained fifteen rows of fifteen matrices each, with six characters omitted from each corner. All of the characters in a row share a single escapement and had to be prepared on the same width. After studying a type family, the letterdrawing office assigned a width of eighteen units to the widest potential characters, with a height to width ratio appropriate to the design. Each of the characters in the roman, italic and bold were then assigned to an available width in discrete units, and a place in a row.

Typefaces don't naturally divide themselves into sets of fifteen

[1]Lawrence Wallis, "Frank Hinman Pierpont: An unsung pioneer of mechanical typesetting," *Electronic Publishing,* 15 July 1994.

characters, with all characters in a set fitting properly into one of eighteen strictly related widths. Letters were moved from width to width and row to row until the scheme was balanced for the machine. The full set of characters was then redrawn until the spacing, color, and shape were properly adjusted to fit the new width assignments. Craftsmanship of a high order was required if the adjustments were not to be visible as irregularities. Pierpont solved the first massive problem. For as long as he lived Monotype fonts were known for good shape, even fit and color.

He was immediately thrown into the second problem, adaptation of typefaces and the building of a Monotype library. After a difficult start with two designs, Miller & Richard's *Modern* and *Old Style* in 1900 and 1901, the early series poured out—thirty-one faces by the start of 1905—one hundred by the end of 1911. All were faithful adaptations of existing designs to the Monotype requirements.

In that year Monotype Series 59 *Veronese* hinted at things to come. Cut for the London publisher J. M. Dent, *Veronese* forms part of the revival of Nicholas Jenson's types started by William Morris with his *Golden Type* in 1890. A single roman lacking an italic, *Veronese* is not a faithful copy, but owes much to ATF *Jenson* and the 1900 *Doves Roman,* with a skillful contribution from the Monotype type drawing office. This distinctive design survived at Monotype for many years as display sizes for *Italian Old Style,* cut the following year.

The change really arrived in 1912 with Series 101, *Imprint,* the first original series designed for the Monotype machine. Morison describes it here as "portentous . . . the first design, not copied or stolen from the typefounders, to establish itself as a standard bookface." The design of a reformed Caslon deliberately envisioned for use on the Monotype by Gerard Meynell, Edward Johnston and J. H. Mason began the second phase, the creative construction of a *Monotype* library of typefaces, ten years before Morison's arrival on the scene. Pierpont's contribution, quality of drawing and fit, is impeccable. Three quarters of a century later *Imprint* retains the status of an industry standard, offered in excellent cuttings by Berthold, Bitstream, Linotype and Monotype.

The experience galvanised Pierpont. Encouraged by that farseeing managing-director and fellow American, Harold Malcolm Duncan, he was off to Antwerp and was back in April 1913 with samples and "historical data" from the Plantin Museum. Monotype's second original typeface, *Plantin*, was released that August, a prompt performance that left little time for scholarly enquiry or reflection. The typeface met with immediate commercial success, and has remained a standard, offered today by Berthold, Bitstream, Linotype and Monotype, Agfa-Compugraphic, Alphatype, Autologic, triple I, Letraset, Scangraphic, Varityper and Visual Graphics.

The serious visitor to the Plantin in those days, browsing through the sixteenth century documents, sooner or later became conscious of a series of vigorous and unusually spirited romans from the hand of an unknown punchcutter. Pierpont recognized the quality of this design, and seized on heavily inked proofs of the *Gros Cicero*. They had been taken off worn type that had been cast in the 1730s for the Moretus. Pierpont accepted the model at hand, although disfigured by J. M. Smit's replacement "a," and produced a typeface softer and heavier than the original, distinguished mainly by the superior quality of color and spacing.

A more complete realization of the design was not to appear for sixty-five years. In the summer of 1939 Ray Nash cast type at the Museum from the *Ascendonica* and identified the cutter as Robert Granjon. The outbreak of war interrupted his progress, which was to lead eventually to the cutting of Matthew Carter's *Galliard,* released by Linotype in 1978, and in which these words are set. Based on careful analysis of Granjon's romans and italics, his character and intentions, *Galliard* revealed what Nash had recognized, an original as brilliant as the designs of John Baskerville.

Pierpont's development of new faces continued with the cutting of a traditional *Caslon* in 1915, and after the War with *Scotch Roman* in 1920 and *Bodoni* in 1921, followed by the *Garamond* of 1922. All

xiii

followed *Plantin* in their solid craft, brisk development and conservative interpretation, and all met with immediate commercial success.

The cutting of *Garamond* followed the visit of an industry deputation, which attended on Duncan to solicit Monotype participation in this popular series, obtainable from ATF since 1917. Duncan was inclining towards an active in-house Monotype program to foresee industry requirements, and he found the means of introducing it in the person of Stanley Morison. Frank Pierpont was enjoying typographic development, the mastery of his chosen craft, the swiftness and efficiency of his straightforward methods for filling customers' requirements, and the quality of the organisation he had created at the Works. One can imagine his reaction at the introduction of this young conscientious objector, provocatively radical, chosen to elaborate and direct the origination of new type designs for a program he had created and managed in detail for nearly a quarter of a century.

Although unable to create an original design himself, Pierpont was a demonstrated master at drawing and adapting them for difficult machines. When designs new to Monotype were requested from the field, with usable models supplied, Pierpont continued with their development himself. So the flow of Monotype adaptations remained in his hands. He polished his ability to discipline unruly originals, notably turning Berthold's end-of-the-century *Ideal Grotesk* into the 1926 *Monotype Grotesques 215 and 216*, and then transforming the Inland Type Foundry's 1911 *Litho Antique* into the 1933 *Monotype Rockwell*.

Morison faced a problem in getting his own faces into production, expressed in his own words in the *Tally:*

> Accordingly the continuity of the plan hinged upon the possibility of counteracting the obstruction of the works by ensuring orders in advance for the matrices that were planned. It was, therefore, peculiarly fortunate that the

typographical adviser to the Corporation should become associated in a similar capacity with the Cambridge Press, headed as it was by a Printer empowered to include or to exclude any typographical equipment that might be rendered available.[2]

Walter Lewis and the CUP provided Morison with support for his program from the highest levels of the industry, support that enabled him to get his ideas into production.

As Typographical Adviser to the Monotype Corporation in London, Morison worked at Monotype House in Fetter Lane, thirty miles from Salfords. He enjoyed the backing of the Managing Director, initially Duncan, followed by Burch, and worked through them as necessary. One can understand his emphasis on controlling the development program in his dealings with Pierpont, autocrat of the works, upon whose skills he so depended. The tensions are portrayed in an unpublished draft of a letter to Cyril Burt from Beatrice Warde written on 22 July 1953, the period when the *Tally* was being prepared.

None of these faces was cut for the Corporation for any other reason than Mr Morison said so and they'd lose him if they didn't obey orders. "Fetter Lane", the seat of the Managing Director until 1939, took on the programme with the same zest and pride, and at least with great faith in S. M. "The Works" on the other hand down at Salfords i.e. Mr Pierpont, a Connecticut engineer, hated S. M. and all he stood for, and was always surly in coming to heel. . . . Pierpont died before the 2nd war but left the works impregnated with his personality. They are wonderful engineers and that's all.[3]

[2]*Tally of Types,* p. 34.
[3]Draft, Beatrice Warde papers in the Morison Collection, Manuscript Collection, University Library, Cambridge.

Morison's own opinion of Pierpont's methods are to be found toward the end of the introduction and most vividly in the chapter on the *Poliphilus*. The two parts of the development program ran side by side, with little contact.

Pierpont's view of Morison might well have been reinforced by Morison's essay in the *Tally* portraying the *Garamond Italic* as *"The Italic of Robert Granjon* / Originally Cut for the Printer of Paris 1530 / First Recut by the Monotype Corporation 1922".* The typeface so described is Jean Jannon's c. 1610 italic in a brisk and faithful recutting in Pierpont style, the pair to the straightforward version of the Jannon roman released as *Monotype Garamond*. The text in the *Tally* actually describes a series of tied characters and swash capitals skillfully based on a characteristically exuberant Granjon model. In January 1923, shortly after release of the *Garamond,* Morison wrote to D. B. Updike about

> the Le Bé fount with its *m* [final] *n* [final] *nt* [ligature] *e* [final] *et* [ligature] *at* [ligature] and other italic ligatures wh. at my requisition are now to be had on the Monotype (English Corp.) for use with their Garamond. In a day or two I hope to send you specimens. I invite your opinion of the face. I hope it is at least an improvement on the A.T.C.'s version. Yours faithfully, Stanley Morison[4]

The wording suggests that these additional italic characters make up Morison's contribution to the *Garamond*, the first typeface in his program. They are used lavishly in the *Tally* to dress up the composition, while lending a strong Granjon flavor to the setting. The original capitals appear sparsely and signal the Jannon origin; the C, F, and R stand out in particular.

The relations between the two men may have also obscured an American contribution to the origin of *Times New Roman*. A similar

[4]Stanley Morison & D. B. Updike, *Selected Correspondence,* David McKitterick ed. (London: Scolar Press, 1980), p. 19.

roman from The Lanston Monotype Company, Number 54 in their development program, anticipates and strongly resembles *Times,* and further study may throw light on the excogitation of the design mentioned by Morison in the *Tally.*

The management of any composing machine manufacturer was familiar with conflicts between engineers and artist/typographers. Few found a Pierpont; most struggled with half-disciplined drawing offices and accepted lower typographic quality, selling machines through speed and price. Those who achieved stable design discipline were faced with paying customers constantly demanding machine versions of every cut of every popular typeface, many of them overlapping duplicates. In the clamor of the first years, Linotype and Monotype were too busy satisfying customers' demands to recognize the benefits of planning typeface design. An innovative program of new designs based on market analysis, scholarship and artistic imagination stood little chance against the rush of proven cash demand provided by raw customers' orders.

The pause of the First World War seemed to draw management's attention to the opportunity. At Mergenthaler in 1915 C. H. Griffith, country printer and Linotype salesman, proposed a rational typographic development program; he was promoted to manage the matrix factory and bring order to a confused library. He retained the best version of each significant design, scrapping duplicates produced to customer orders; he examined the typographic requirements of each market for Linotype machines and rebuilt the library with original typefaces designed to better serve each of them.

Seven years later The Monotype Corporation, London, engaged Morison as Typographical Adviser for a similar purpose. Mergenthaler had employed Griffith to pilot a program and improve craftsmanship, resolving both aspects of the problem. Faced with two powerful but clashing personalities in Morison and Pierpont, Monotype took the unusual course of institutionalising the conflict between them, and out of opposition produced a brilliant result. Morison founded the Monotype's creative growth on the deep, original historical scholarship so evident in the *Tally* and augmented by his close cooperation with Eric Gill. Pierpont could be counted on to provide the necessary craftsmanship.

Understanding the situation at Monotype in those years illuminates many aspects of the *Tally*—Morison's preference for exploring new designs with outside designers and hand punchcutters, the sections on *Garamond* and the *Granjon Italic,* on *Poliphilus* and *Bembo*, the mix-up between *Fournier* and *Barbou*—and may illuminate the origin of *Times New Roman*. The Monotype releases that do not appear in the *Tally* are by and large the typefaces with which Morison was not concerned: the 1926 *Monotype Grotesques* and the 1933 *Monotype Rockwell* were clearly the work of Pierpont; yet the thoughtful quality of his adaptations of *Ideal Grotesque* and *Litho Antique* seem to show Morison's influence. In 1928 Pierpont cut *Othello*, an unauthorised version of *Neuland*. By 1936 its place in the line was taken by Berthold Wolpe's *Albertus,* undertaken at Morison's instigation.

We forget, and perhaps the world never fully understood, the sum of the difficulties facing the ambitious manufacturers of early composing machines. We tend to underrate the labor of tailoring typefaces to fit stubborn and difficult machines, while maintaining an apparently easy elegance of shape and fit. By comparison our common digital problem of intelligently scaling and rasterising outlines for screens, printers and imagesetters are simple and direct. As manufacturers accept a handful of digital formats for fonts as standards that run industry-wide we can forget the anxiety of depending upon the offerings of a single equipment manufacturer for all of our typographic requirements. We find that once again we can purchase fonts for our equipment from a variety of sources, not the least of which is Monotype, a firm that continues to provide the fonts that poured out over half a century ago in the unsurpassed outburst of typographic development chronicled here.

In the *Tally* we have an insider's account of the brilliant, innovative and vital side of the powerful double-barreled program that Stanley Morison and Fetter Lane, Frank Pierpont and The Works,

Walter Lewis and the Cambridge University Press all conspired to develop. As Typographical Adviser to the Monotype Corporation, Cambridge University Press, and Times Newspapers Limited, Morison's typographic accomplishments remain unsurpassed. We can surmise the importance of Pierpont's contribution in craftsmanship and manufacturing judgement. The quality and variety of the typefaces in the program remain as useful to our present digital world as they were when cast in typemetal sixty years ago. Combining creative typeface design with the realities of manufacturing equipment and matrices in the first half of this century was never easy. In all probability, the extraordinary success of this ultimately cooperative effort is perhaps the lasting monument of the management genius of Harold Malcolm Duncan and William Burch.

Careful reading of the *Tally* can leave the reader with a sense of *lacunae*, of significant things left unsaid. Indication of the other half of the program would be at best incomplete without access to that vast repository of information on the craft, industry and art of the typographic tradition, the Saint Bride Printing Library, and the guidance of its Librarian, James Mosley, from whose enquiring mind and through whose collection other Monotype realities will surely take on shape, form and detail.

MIKE PARKER
San Diego, December 1998

Asterisks refer to notes on
pp. 127–133

INTRODUCTION
BY STANLEY MORISON
REVISED & AMPLIFIED BY
P. M. HANDOVER

Technical changes in the nineteenth century operated with a speed that made discrimination impossible. Machines were employed for every kind of work irrespective of its right, universally admitted in the eighteenth century, to treatment as an aspect of art. The types used in the printing trade had, since the fifteenth century, been cast from matrices struck from punches which had been engraved directly by the hands of goldsmiths and other chasers and metalworkers. These were the men who were responsible for the craftsmanship, in the creative sense of the word, and for the utility of the design; for its shapes, its measurements, its economic value, its desirability as a reflection of genius. And 'genius' is not too high a term for the work of some of these goldsmith-punchcutters. Benvenuto Cellini certainly knew what he was talking about when he referred to the seals cut by one of them as from the hand of 'the great Lautizio'.

The later professionalization of this work on an independent craft basis, in accordance with the expansion of the art and mystery into a trade and a craft, brought no essential change in the technique; punches were still engraved by hand during the nineteenth century. As Talbot Baines Reed, himself a typefounder, remarked in 1887, the description of typecutting in Paris given by Fournier le jeune in 1764 might have served as an up-to-date manual in the mid-nineteenth century.

In 1885 in Milwaukee a punch-cutting machine was invented by Linn Boyd Benton, a master typefounder. This was the machine that was destined to disorganize the connection of artist-engravers with the printing trade, to disperse the punch-cutters and to destroy the basis of design upon which typography had rested since its invention in the 1440s.

In 1886, the year after Benton had registered a British patent for his engraving machine, a capital event occurred. In the office of the *New York Tribune* a machine arranged lines of matrices by the tapping of a keyboard and then pumped lead into the completed lines. Ottmar Mergenthaler's 'Linotype' had worked successfully. Five years later an American journalist named Harold Malcolm Duncan was able to make in *Paper and Press* the first formal announcement that Tolbert Lanston had succeeded with his 'Monotype' in separating the functions of keyboarding from casting, and had thereby produced a machine setting not single *lines* like Mergenthaler's Linotype but single *types*.

The Benton engraving machine was a typographical invention as fundamental as the mould of Gutenberg (*c.* 1440), the stereotype plate of Johann Müller (1708), the steam press of König and Bauer (1814). Neither the Linotype nor the Monotype would have been possible without the Benton invention. It solved the composing machines' essential need for the mass production of punches.

At this time, too, the typefounders of the United States adopted a new system of measuring their type-bodies. Although many of the old names, particularly those deriving from liturgical printing, were common to most European countries, they were not always attached to bodies of even approximately the same size; for instance, German *text* was substantially larger than Dutch *text*. A more troublesome discrepancy was that between body sizes regarded as the same: a German *tertia* might take the same place in the range of founts as an English *great primer*, a French *gros romain* or a Dutch *text*, all being approximately 16-point, but none was necessarily exactly the same size as the other. In 1694 the French had envisaged a reform with sizes mathematically based and newly named (*Louvre, Bignon, Phély-peaux, Pontchartrain, Louis*) but the project was abandoned. A rationalization of the old bodies on a system akin to the point was anticipated by Pierre Simon Fournier in 1737 and perfected by François Ambroise Didot in 1775, but they failed to break down the national preferences for different nomenclature and measurement. When the point system was established in 1886 on an American scale the effect was revolutionary. Henceforth the designing of faces for machine composition could be grounded on a single universal unit of measurement, the point, although in fact the Anglo-American and Didot systems still run in parallel.

In 1900 a separate company was set up in England to develop the invention of Tolbert Lanston; Harold Malcolm Duncan, who had become Lanston's friend and technical adviser, was its first managing director. Not only were the keyboards and casters to be manufactured at the factory then established at Horley but the punches and matrices were to be cut and stamped there too. This factory was ruled by F. H. Pierpont, an engineer who had worked for a company manufacturing machines for slug composition. The first designs were naturally those already proven by the foundries to be most in demand, and series 1 of the new Lanston Monotype Corporation was therefore a 'Modern', since throughout the nineteenth century in books and newspapers the Modern face had reigned supreme and virtually unchallenged.

MODERN NOS. 1 & 7

First cut by Miller & Richard and recut by
the Monotype Corporation in 1900 and 1902

One of the advantages of setting the single types cast on the Monotype machine was that letters could be freely kerned. Modern series 1 so reduced the kerns on letters like f and j that they might have been designed for slug matrices. On the other hand, the face demonstrated the facility with which small condensed letters with fine hairlines could be cut in small sizes on the pantographic engraving machine.

'Modern face' was established in France when the *romain du roi* was cut by Philippe Grandjean on instructions (supported by some engraved specimens) given to him by the commission appointed by the *Académie des Sciences* in 1692. The influence of this letter upon the Italian printer and punchcutter Giambattista Bodoni was to be great (see pp. 30–2). In France the Didot family of typefounders chiefly developed the Modern face and in the period between the Pierre Didot *ainé* specimen of 1819 and those of *Firmin Didot frères* in the 1830s they were performing upon it the operations that led William Morris later so vehemently to condemn the Moderns: the vicious thickening and thinning which made them difficult to read, the lateral compression that was the result of commercial exigency, and the basic crudity that was inherent when craftsmanship was ignored.

During the nineteenth century the Scottish and English founders moved away from the extreme contrast of thick and thin to lighter types that had a grey effect on the page. Thus in 1834 the Edinburgh typefounder William Miller announced new founts, explicitly fitted 'for MACHINE-PRINTING', that were lighter, sharper versions of their earlier Modern, and by the 1860s their Moderns had been further lightened. For instance in 1834 they showed new breviers, nos. 6 and 9 to 13; by 1863 they were showing nos. 18, 20, 21, 22, 28 in the same size.

Monotype series 1 was based on the weight of the middle period rather than the extreme greyness of the later founts. This was a style of letter to which thousands of readers of Cambridge Press books were accustomed, and consequently it was bought by the Press when the first Monotypes were installed in 1913. At that time considerable pains were taken to compose it to look as much as possible like the founder's type on which it had been based. The 11-point, for instance, should have been 9¾ set but at the

Press it was—and still is—10 set, so that it had the same effect as the Miller & Richard 4-nick small pica which it was intended to replace.

In 1902 the Corporation cut the less economical Modern series 7, based on series 1 but with more generous proportions and technically superior. This was the Modern that was bought for use in *The Times* in 1908, when Lord Northcliffe installed Monotypes at Printing House Square in place of the Kastenbeins. The choice was made because series 7 resembled the broad Miller & Richard Modern previously in use; such faces were preferred by newspapers for their economic advantage in the classified advertising. The Cambridge Press also bought series 7 in 1913. Both series 1 and series 7 were supplied with a very wide variety of peculiar, including mathematical and scientific sorts, and with Greek and script founts of allied design and set. Because of this richness series 7 has still not been supplanted at the Press and is not likely to be so long as hot-metal type is used.

It was the Moderns that in the nineteenth century had already been cut with the special sorts needed for science and mathematics and thus their position was firmly entrenched against the Caslon old-face revival after 1840. This appeared to concern only the printers of literary classics or of devotional books or poetry. The *Euclid* (1847) printed in Caslon by the Chiswick Press was a solitary departure and justified by the antiquity of the text rather than by the scientific content. The Victorian eye had become accustomed to the regularity of the Modern letter, to the neatness of its fit and the refinement of its cutting. Consequently the Caslon revived by William Pickering and the Chiswick Press in 1840 was by contrast even more irregular and less shapely than it would have seemed to either the eighteenth- or the twentieth-century reader. The original founts of Chiswell Street (described on pp. 24–27) needed to be 'improved'.

OLD STYLE
First cut by Miller & Richard in 1858 and
recut by the Monotype Corporation in 1900

'The faces which were cut in the early part of the last century are now unpleasing both to the eye of the critic and to the general reader, on account of their inequality of *size* and consequent irregularity of *ranging*'—so the Edinburgh typefounders Miller & Richard commented in 1860. Two years earlier they had ventured on the first two sizes of a modernized Caslon and by 1860 had completed a series in which they had 'endeavoured to avoid the objectionable peculiarities, while retaining the distinctive characteristics of the mediaeval letters'.

Old Style, as they named their 'mediaeval' letter first cut in 1858, can fairly be described as an invention. What in Caslon did not conform to Victorian ideas of typographical rectitude had been cast out. Even swash letters were not included. Eyes used to sharpness of cut and regularity of letter-width found both in Old Style. Most important of all, the stress was vertical. Here was a respectable cousin of the Didot Modern.

Variations described either as Old Style or—so great was the authority of Miller & Richard—as Mediaeval were cut not only in this island but abroad, and even the Chiswick Press bought founts. The success of Old Style was not undeserved, for the design was practical for commercial purposes in a manner similar to the several 'legibility' faces designed for newspaper composition in the 1920s and 1930s. The lack of pedigree did not worry the Victorians. In April 1890 Talbot Baines Reed told the Society of Arts how the 'mediaevals' had been 'embellished...with the delicate tapers and hairlines of the modern school'. The dexterity in typefounding so displayed had his approval: 'This opportune return to the past, I venture to think, is a hopeful sign for the future.' The Cambridge Press shared the general enthusiasm and relied upon Miller & Richard's Old Style until the installation of the Monotype enabled it to take advantage of Monotype Old Style, series 2, cut in 1900 on the same model.

Even in 1858 Old Style had been contrived to display the resources of the Industrial Revolution. By 1900 the place of the skilled craftsman having full responsibility for the form of the letters destined to appear on the printed page had been taken by engineers and inventors of machinery, attended by syndicates of capitalists and financiers. For such the economic exploitation of an invention was the single desideratum, and printing as an artistic skill did not exist. It was precisely this destruction of art by industry that Morris set himself to combat.

In 1888 Emery Walker had delivered the lecture on printing to the Arts and Crafts Exhibition Society that inspired Morris to make a new type. An anti-renaissance man himself, Morris raised the humanist cry 'ad fontes'. In 1891 the Golden type, the first fount to be used for Morris's Kelmscott 'private' press, was cast by Reed from the punches of Edward Prince. In 1892 Morris acquired the assistance, as secretary, of Sydney Cockerell. In 1898 Cockerell was introduced by W. R. Lethaby to Edward Johnston, who was studying calligraphy at the fountain-head —the British Museum.

It is to these men, Morris, Walker, Cockerell, Lethaby, Johnston, that we owe the recovery of the right making of letters in both calligraphy and typography. Reed died at the age of forty-one. His first school story, *The Adventures of a Three-Guinea Watch*, was published when he was twenty-eight, and his *History of the Old English Letter Foundries*, so remarkable an achievement for its time (and later admirably brought up to date by A. F. Johnson), was published in 1887, when its author was thirty-five. He was the first honorary secretary of the Bibliographical Society, and it may well have been he who persuaded Morris to address the Society on the subject of the 'Ideal Book' on 19 June 1893, in which year Reed died. Had he lived it is certain that, with his practical trade knowledge, he would have accelerated the process by which the immediate 'aims' of the Kelmscott Press became understood by an audience far more numerous and widespread than the subscribers to *The Glittering Plain* and the *Chaucer*. Reed could have rendered these 'aims' apt to be handed on to future generations of typographical craftsmen; thereby to have wedded the artistry of the 'private' to the industry of the 'trade' press. Lamentable as Reed's early death was, the movement did not languish, thanks mainly to Walker.*

In 1899 Johnston, having taken in his fill of calligraphy at the fountain-head, began to teach at the Central School of Arts and Crafts in London. After Reed's death, the effect on the trade of this recovery of knowledge was felt principally in Germany, the classical land of printing and possessor of more typefoundries than any other country in the world. The German artists, active from 1900 to 1925 under the impulse of the British Arts and Crafts Movement, and of the 'Münchener Renaissance' style that was its contemporary, produced many new designs. Yet few showed promise of satisfying British printers desirous of providing themselves with new book-faces. They required a type which, while being new, could be relied upon to be in use for a number of years. Judged by this standard there was only one, out of the scores then cut, of the new German book-types that has justified itself—

the roman and italic
cut by the Bauer Typefoundry in 1925
from the designs of Emil Rudolf Weiss.

Another factor of prime importance was that the work of these artists was not designed with the right mechanical means in view. Despite the efficiency of German industry as a whole, mechanization in the composing rooms of houses specializing in book-printing had proceeded relatively slowly. Newspaper houses apart, German printing continued to rely upon composing by hand. Hence, it was not foreseen by German artists that mechanical composition would, sooner or later, take first place.

At this time the typefounders were the beneficiaries as well as the champions of hand composition. Also they led in the creation of types appropriate for advertising and publicity, branches of the trade in which novelty and display are requisite. The book sizes of novel types obtained considerable use—for a time. There is, or was, outside Britain a tendency to like what was new for the sake of its novelty. Thus, in sum, German book-faces designed for private presses became strongly personal and those for publicity purposes very striking.

The situation was not dissimilar in France and the United States. From the last-named country came the final transmogrification of Caslon, the triumph of Old Style: Cheltenham Old Style, designed by an architect, Bertram Goodhue. The long-worshipped contrast of thick and thin strokes and the tapered serifs were abandoned in favour of even tone and blunt serifs; A was startlingly sheared and g strikingly contorted. Cheltenham was to enjoy a popularity that has possibly not been equalled except by Times New Roman and Univers. Like the latter it was an all-purpose type, and the first to be made. No other face was at that time available in so great a range of normal, wide and condensed weights, all readily identifiable. It was originally cut by American Type Founders, and was quickly reproduced on the hot-metal composing machines and used for books, newspapers and general printing.

IMPRINT
Cut by the Monotype Corporation
for *The Imprint* in 1912

Among the new generation of the Arts and Crafts Movement, then led by Lethaby, there were dissidents who found the private press faces unsuitable for general trade use. Friends of Edward Johnston, such as Gerard Meynell of the Westminster Press and J. H. Mason, director of printing at the Central School, believed that what was needed was a face as generally useful as Old Style series 2 but more distinguished in pedigree and less anaemic in appearance. In particular they saw the need for a face that would print well on the coated paper needed for half-tone illustration. They proposed to combine the distinction of the private press types with the practical needs of the commercial trade.

Their convictions extended beyond type design: they also planned a periodical that would raise printing 'to its worthy place among the crafts'. Meynell was not only a printer but an energetic propagandist, gifted like others of his family with a lively mind and artistic tastes; Mason had worked with Cobden-Sanderson at the Doves Press. In collaboration with Johnston and Ernest Jackson, an expert in lithography, they would undertake a new journal for the trade. In August Meynell wired Johnston: 'Have chosen the simplest title—*The Imprint*'. The new type designed to the specification of Meynell and his associates was appropriately christened Imprint Old Face. The matrices which the Corporation had been instructed to prepare arrived at the Westminster Press on 13 December 1912 and no. 1 of *The Imprint* appeared in January. The editors referred only to a newly designed type which they were confident would bear comparison with the best of the privately owned types and did not discuss details or general principles. It was clear, however, that they had returned to pre-1858 and considered a reformed Caslon. Thus the letter width of Imprint is more regular than original Caslon, though not so monotonous as Old Style. The letters fitted together well in the manner of a Modern. Details such as the absence of a lower serif on C were shared with Old Style but the stress of Imprint was not vertical and this effectively distinguished it from all the inheritance of the Miller & Richard invention. The originality of Imprint lay in the x-height and the weight, both more generous than in original Caslon. Indeed, when Imprint and Caslon were printed for comparison on coated paper it might be seen that they had little in common.

Since the editorial policy was to improve general standards, Imprint was offered to the trade without restriction. The Cambridge Press, unfortunately, did not see the potentialities of a face that only became one of its chief props after 1917 when Bruce Rogers had pointed out the merits in his report to the Syndics on the Press's typography.* Nor did the Corporation attach importance to a face that it had been asked to prepare; it made no effort to assist the journal, which began to fail after eight issues and which closed with the ninth.

The importance of Imprint was that the design had been originated for mechanical composition. It was the first design, not copied or stolen from the typefounders, to establish itself as a standard book-face. Its success as a type and as a commercial product proved that in the future all types, good or bad, for manual or mechanical composition, would be drawn and pantographically cut by engraving machines. It was plain, also, that the typefounders were, and would be, unable to provide for the needs of machine composition.

Thus the adoption in 1912 by Gerard Meynell, Edward Johnston and J. H. Mason of Monotype composition for *The Imprint* was portentous. And it was important that the type design was not concocted by Meynell, Johnston and Mason on a piece of bristol board. They eschewed novelty. What they decided was to redraw an eighteenth-century face that had been stamped with the approval of no mean judge in such matters: Thomas Frognall Dibdin.* It cannot be doubted that Dibdin would have welcomed the recutting in terms of machine composition, and would not have despised the new edition of a portion of the *Bibliographical Decameron* which the editors included in *The Imprint*. The significance of series 101 could not be missed; the founding of types according to the old system was a dying industry. It might die by inches or picas or points, but doomed it was. Book composition in the future, like newspaper composition already, would be done on machines.

PLANTIN
Cut by Claude Garamond, c. 1550, and recut by the Monotype Corporation in 1913

The example of Imprint as a dual-purpose face, equally suited to antique and coated papers, encouraged the works manager at Horley, F. H. Pierpont, to consider the provision by the Corporation of another design intended for printing on 'art' paper. A visit to Antwerp, prompted by his managing director's interest in printing history, gave him the idea for the basic design. At Antwerp he saw at the Plantin Museum the unrivalled collection of sixteenth-century punches and matrices used by Christopher Plantin, who had been active as a printer in the city 1555–89.* Pierpont also saw the magnificent commemorative volumes prepared by Max Rooses, the then Curator, and the specimens prepared by recasting the ancient types.

A keen technician like Pierpont could find in the Museum examples and documentation of the various stages in the manufacture of a design and it was enthralling. To reinforce his interest there was the enthusiasm of Rooses, who was then working on the expanded resetting in princely format of his *Christopher Plantin, imprimeur anversois* for publication in 1914. Pierpont bore away photographs and reproductions, including examples of Robert Granjon's *Gros Cicero*, of which a set of matrices exists at the Plantin Museum. Plantin himself never used these matrices, which were only acquired by the Moretus family after 1652, but he mixed some of these Granjon letters with others from Garamond's St Augustin to make a large-faced pica.

Under Pierpont's direction an adaptation of this sixteenth-century type was drawn and pantographically cut at the Monotype works. In adapting it for contemporary needs the draughtsmen and mechanics at Salfords once again showed that intelligent understanding which they displayed when creating Monotype

Imprint in 1912 from an Old Face model. Descenders were shortened considerably and ascenders slightly in order to give compact setting, yet the preservation of a generous x-height secured for Plantin a legibility evident even in 6-point. The serifs were strongly bracketed and thus able to resist the pressure of stereotyping, and a differentiation between the thick and thin strokes in favour of the former gave a rich effect that was more characteristic of Jenson than Garamond but countered the light impression necessary in the printing of half-tones. Several letters were rationalized, for instance the counters of a and e were enlarged, so that when Plantin had to be printed on cheap paper there were no potential ink traps.

Indeed, when Pierpont had finished the design had perhaps as much in common with a nineteenth-century Clarendon as with a sixteenth-century Garamond. Although the classic old-face text design was preserved in the structure, the strength and colour required by a face for display and jobbing were imposed. The combination was both deliberate and successful. After the War Francis Meynell's Pelican and C. W. Hobson's Cloister Press, both typographically influential, adopted Monotype Plantin, and it rapidly gained ground in the advertising agencies as its qualities in newspaper reproduction were recognized. Only in recent years, as the grotesques have become dominant, has the slogan 'When in doubt, use Plantin' lost power.

Bruce Rogers, in his report on the typography of the Cambridge Press, considered that series 110 was 'not generally suitable' for bookwork, but because of its value for catalogue setting and other semi-jobbing work he recommended that stocks should be increased. The design was, however, attractively used by the Press in 1920 for *Beauty and the Beast* by S. A. McDowall.

Pierpont had not intended a period face. It was Francis Meynell who saw how the sixteenth-century pedigree could be exploited. He persuaded the Corporation to add tied sorts, even an *in*, and in 1918 showed these in *The Best of Both Worlds*, a selection of the poems of Henry Vaughan and Andrew Marvell. After the foundation of the Nonesuch Press he further induced the Corporation to cut for him special long descenders, so that for the Nonesuch Herodotus (printed at Cambridge in 1935), 10-point Plantin, leaded 2 points, had p, g, j, q, and y cut on a 12-point body.

At the time when Rogers was writing his report he thought more highly of Plantin Light, series 113, of which one size only (12-point) had been cut when he wrote. Series 113 was a mechanical adaptation of the normal weight, cut to meet the publishers' demand for a text face less black than series 110. Till the early 1920s it usefully filled a gap, for no other sixteenth-century face had then been cut by the Corporation, a deficiency supplied, as described later, after 1922.

CASLON
Cut by William Caslon and first shown in
his specimen of 1734; recut by the
Monotype Corporation in 1915

The example of typographers such as Bernard Newdigate during the first decade of the twentieth century made Caslon so popular that when Rogers was quitting the United States for these shores in 1915 he was warned by a friend that he was visiting 'a Caslon-ridden country'. That the types of William Caslon I (1692–1766) enjoyed at this period an esteem far greater than during their creator's lifetime—and that had not been inconsiderable—was due to their being the only real Old Face that was readily available from English typefounders to those printers and publishers who wished to escape from Modern.

Caslon had issued his first specimen sheet in 1734, although his foundry had been in existence since 1720. Originally an engraver and chaser of metal, he was in that year engaged by the Society for Promoting Christian Knowledge to cut a fount of Arabic for missionary printing. The quality of his work was recognized by the London printer William Bowyer and Caslon proceeded with roman letters such as the pica roman, finished by 1725. His considerable output, marked by a precision that far exceeded that of any predecessor in Britain, ensured a success that the types did not altogether warrant. Caslon was the first British typefounder of consequence; he was almost the last cutter of an Old Face and his work was necessarily somewhat removed from the models of the sixteenth century.

What was then fashionable in Britain was the Dutch Old Face cut by Christopher van Dyck between 1648 and 1670. These were the letters that Caslon reproduced. The sturdiness and the open counters, as well as a certain narrowness prefigured in some of Robert Granjon's italics, were reproduced from the Dutch in Caslon's larger sizes of roman and italic. The alternative founts that he or his son cut for text setting were a smaller rather than a condensed letter.

By the time Caslon came to Van Dyck, however, British hand-writing had been transformed by the round-hand script popu-larized by such writing masters as James Seddon, John Snell and George Shelley. British business and commerce was conducted in round-hand and a British bill of lading was recognizable across seven seas for a distinctive calligraphy. Hence Caslon interpreted his Dutch models with what had become a native roundness and it was this quality that secured for his founts later tributes as 'English', 'comfortable', 'friendly'. Because of British commer-cial domination Caslon could ignore the influence of Continental designs—the economy that was gaining ground in Germany and Holland, the sharpness and contrast so admired in France after Grandjean cut the *romain du roi*. The reputation of the Caslon foundry sanctified in this country for another generation a tradi-tional Old Face that elsewhere was being hurried, it was then thought, to extinction.

At the time when the Monotype Corporation was established

in England the typefounders were making money out of their Caslon founts and the Corporation in competition cut series 20 in 1903 as an Old Face based on a size of original Caslon. As Rogers remarked in his 1917 report, series 20 was 'a very close approximation of Caslon Old Face'. It had however the disadvantage that all the founts were repetitions of a single original size. Three years later the Corporation tried again with series 45, marketed as Old Face. With series 20 as the model there was now a deliberate attempt to impose upon the earlier cutting what was in the opinion of the engineers one of the principal virtues of a machine: uniformity. Thus the correct unit values were given to all the sorts.

The series had a moderate success and the Cambridge Press in 1914 bought three sizes, but there was no enthusiasm for a face that had been cut specifically for machine-setting. The rational approach of the Monotype engineers, that the potential superiority in certain respects of mechanical engraving ought to be exploited, was not shared by the trade in general, where the preference was rather for machine-setting that looked as if it had been hand-composed. Rogers considered series 45 'the least satisfactory' of the Monotype faces at the Press and he preferred series 20, which had been bought in 1915 and was therefore to him the 'newer series'. This was used for the first volumes of the 'New Shakespeare' which he designed.

The production of Imprint had done little to satisfy publishers who wanted a genuine Old Face; it was neither quaint nor irregular and had no value in 'period' typography. Printers such as R. & R. Clark of Edinburgh, with big orders for which Caslon was specified, were obliged to continue with hand-setting. On that firm, however, the need to mechanize was urgent, since among their customers was G. B. Shaw, who once declared, 'I'll stick to Caslon until I die'. Soon after Plantin had appeared William Maxwell, then Secretary and already Grand Vizier of R. & R. Clark, impressed upon the Corporation that a Caslon should be cut to look as much as possible like a founder's version. The first sizes of another series, 128, were ready in 1915.

It was unfortunate that Maxwell was impatiently awaiting his matrices while the Corporation was being confronted by the technical difficulties of a face richer in kerned letters than had hitherto been attempted at the works or by any hot-metal composing-machine company. The Monotype version consequently bears the scars of hurried workmanship. There were not merely inconsistencies within the range of founts, for instance in T, but a failure to interpret faithfully the original; individual letters, particularly g and *g*, were hardly recognizable as 'Caslon'. The alphabet fitted together well but in composition the result was less happy, although this was due to the adherence of the Corporation to the command to reproduce a face of which the original punches had been cut by hand.

The provision of series 128 enabled R. & R. Clark to complete J. W. Fortescue's *History of the British Army* for Macmillan on the machine after several volumes had been set by hand, and the Cambridge Press completed Rogers's New Shakespeare in series 128 after using series 20 for the first four volumes; but the attraction of the face lay mainly in the variety of swash letters with which it had been provided.

SCOTCH ROMAN
Cut by Richard Austin c. 1812, and recut as series 46 and 137 by the Monotype Corporation in 1906 and 1920

The description 'Scotch roman' has been applied to various founts made in the early nineteenth century by the Miller foundry of Edinburgh. William Miller, who had been foreman in Alexander Wilson's foundry in Glasgow, issued his earliest surviving type specimen in 1813, one year after the appearance of Wilson's 'modern cut' types. According to T. C. Hansard (*Typographia*,

p. 361) most of the founts of both foundries were executed by Richard Austin,* with so great a degree of similarity between Miller's letter and Wilson's 'as to require minute inspection to distinguish one from the other'.

In 1789 Austin's style had been distinctively modern, as can be seen from his cutting of Bell (p. 87); but his style had become decidedly conservative by 1812. From that date the types issued by the Scottish founders were characterized by broad proportions and full colour; they also displayed generously bracketed serifs, a feature which Austin defended in the preface to his own specimen issued in 1819. Two features which attracted English printers towards these types were succinctly expressed by Hansard, who attributed the popularity of Scotch types 'partly to the superiority of their metal, and partly to their resumption of the old principle of shaping type'. (He could have added a third and most compelling feature—the lower price of types made in Scotland.)

The term 'Scotch' was first applied to type in America, and it does not seem to have been used in England until c. 1920. The American printer and historian T. L. De Vinne believed that it originated with S. N. Dickinson, who imported matrices for his new Boston foundry from Alexander Wilson & Co. This face was 'a small, neat, round letter, with long ascenders and not noticeably condensed or compressed'. De Vinne further claimed that the first complete series of the 'Scotch-face' was produced by James Conner of New York; but it can be seen from Conner's specimen of 1859 that his 'Scotch-type' was light, condensed and virtually indistinguishable from other contemporary faces produced in America and Scotland.

When the Monotype Corporation issued series 46 in 1906, it was labelled 'Pica Old Face No. 3' (the name Scotch roman was substituted after 1936). This series was not cut with as much skill and judgement as was later shown by the Monotype works in cutting the Imprint and Plantin types described on pp. 19–24, nor was series 46 based on a single prototype. Nevertheless it has several features in common with a Pica shown by Miller in his specimen of 1813.

After 1900 the name 'Scotch roman' was increasingly used in America to describe a particular series of types, mostly cast from old matrices and sold by Miller & Richard to the publishers T. & A. Constable Ltd of Edinburgh. Because the first book in which these types were used by Constable in 1882 was a revision of Dryden's works, the types were named 'Dryden'. The most distinctive size was the Pica, shown in Miller's specimen of 1813 as the 'New Pica Roman, No. 2'. The same type appears in Miller & Richard's specimen of c. 1909 as '12 point Old No. 2', but the 8, 10 and 11-point sizes were labelled 'Old No. 3 Series'. So it is easy to understand why 'Pica Old Face No. 3' was the description given to Series 46 12-point when it came on to the market in 1906.

A few years earlier the Mergenthaler Linotype Company in America had cut an accurate copy of the Miller type which they called '12 point Scotch'. By 1915 it had been completed in a full range of sizes, all of them sensitive adaptations of the originals. By contrast neither series 46 nor the later and more loosely fitted series 137 cut by the Monotype Corporation faithfully recaptures the fine qualities of Miller's prototypes. For in series 46 the mistake was made of cutting every size to match the pica model, whereas fidelity demanded respect for the subtle variations of design in the different original sizes.

Of all the sizes cut by Miller, the pica was the most distinctive: it was a broad letter with very heavy and idiosyncratic capitals. The C and G have slightly canted upper serifs, and a distinct slant to the stress of the curves. Nothing like these capitals appears in any of the other sizes of Miller's romans, nor of Wilson's; but curiously enough these same features are to be seen in the series of Two-line Pearl Titling Capitals cut by Wilson, and also cut by Miller. Not only did Miller show these capitals in his specimen of 1813 as Titling Capitals; in the same specimen the identical letters are shown as capitals for his 'New Pica Roman, no. 2'.

In revising the pica for use by Constables, these idiosyncrasies were retained by Miller & Richard, but they recut the letters S, e and t to meet the current taste. Unhappily they also selected an odd combination of heavy capitals and light lower-case which had only appeared once—in a specimen book of 1814. The result is a very curious type in which neither roman nor italic capitals quite match the lower-case.

BODONI

Cut by Giambattista Bodoni, c. 1767, and recut by
the Monotype Corporation, 1921–28

Scotch Roman was an individual, native version of the Continental modern face; Edinburgh and Glasgow had paid slight attention to Paris and Parma, so that their founts had comparatively little in common with those of the Italian Giambattista Bodoni (1740–1813). The Scotch Modern as it evolved during the nineteenth century was primarily a text face, intended to be economic but legible in cheap printing produced at comparatively high speed. The varieties of Modern created by Bodoni were by contrast more successful in large sizes, heavily leaded and well inked, printed with care on good white paper.

After an apprenticeship in type-cutting and printing at the Vatican printing house Bodoni in 1768 took charge of the ducal printing house at Parma and there he remained for the rest of his life, printing 'fine editions' from type, the punches of which he had (he admitted) lovingly perfected. His first designs were respectful imitations of Fournier, described on pp. 75–80, and the French influence dominated the office at Parma. After 1771 he increasingly developed a style of his own and by 1788 he had cut a considerable number of founts which were displayed in a monumental folio issued in that year. However, this later Parma style

30

and the faces Bodoni adopted from 1780 have no practical merits and owe their interest solely to Bodoni's adoption of the Jansenist heresy, which found expression in the austere, undecorated, not to say bleak, style of the books he printed.

Apart from the direction of the ducal printing house, Bodoni had his own foundry, where his brother cast alphabets which he also supplied to other printers. Thus, when he cut no fewer than ten vareties of *filosofia*, and made a similar lavish provision in other text sizes, he was not impelled by the need to sell what printers needed. The cutting of so many variants was a particular hobby of Bodoni's; four or five was the usual limit in the eighteenth century—Fournier, for instance, cut no more than normal, *gros oeil, petit oeil, serré, goût Hollandois*. Bodoni minutely varied his weight, his extruders and his serifs as well as condensing or expanding, in order to ensure that he could obtain precisely the effect in printing that he wished in different volumes. Yet all the designs were variants of a basic Modern letter form.

His last specimen book in two quarto volumes, quite different from his earlier *Manuale Tipografico*, did not appear until five years after his death, his widow having laboured to produce a worthy memorial. Bodoni's monumental work, his stately office and his prolific output of exotics and scripts, in addition to romans and italics in a dozen varieties and in barely detectable gradations, ensured for him in his lifetime and after a European reputation.

Sooner or later in the twentieth century every foundry and hot-metal composing-machine company was to cut a version of Bodoni and the Corporation did not lag behind, the 12-point of series 135 being ready in 1921. Inevitably there was a wide variation between the designs labelled Bodoni that were marketed in Italy, Britain and the United States, the possible models being so numerous. The Corporation chose a general rendering, perhaps more rigid than the master's own work. It eschewed his more extreme letters, the pronounced tail to R, the g which looked as if it had received a blow in the midriff, and alternative sorts were provided for his favourite highly calligraphic *v* and *w*. Series 135 was a true Bodoni in that it looked best well leaded and did not print well on coated paper. The potentialities of the larger sizes of the black upper-case were however soon exploited by the advertising agencies.

Such was the type-cutting performance of the Lanston Monotype Corporation, showing very little originality, up to 1922, when a plan was laid before the managing director. It was intended as a programme of typographical design, rational, systematic, and corresponding effectively with the foreseeable needs of printing; and it involved the expenditure of a good deal of money and the acceptance of risks that had never been undertaken by a type-composing-machine company. Harold Malcolm Duncan, then managing director of the Corporation, accepted it for two reasons: because, as an educated man, a former technical journalist and editor of *Paper and Press* of Philadelphia, he had a good grasp of the history of the art; as a business man, he believed that the idea was feasible. The Corporation, after long years of poverty, had begun to prosper. It should make a contribution to the invention rendered beautiful, as well as useful, by Gutenberg, Fust and Schoeffer in Mainz; Jenson and Aldus in Venice; Colines and Garamond in Paris; Plantin and Granjon in Antwerp; and other illustrious masters. During 1922, then, the author of this book accepted the post of typographical adviser to the Monotype Corporation on the understanding that the matrix-cutting and publicity programme he had tabulated would be proceeded with immediately.

The plan began with the cutting of the so-called Garamond face, the first size of which was completed in 1922, before Harold Malcolm Duncan unhappily died. It would have been in perfect accord with precedent and prudence if Duncan's successor had thought twice before authorizing the complete fulfilment of the plan accepted by his predecessor. It is not in the normal course of business for successive managing directors to be equally conscious of their business's rise to institutional status, with a responsibility to the public for the designs it may make and sell. Rather it was probable that the new managing director, facing the post-war depression, would more keenly feel his responsibility to the shareholders for the payment of dividends upon the capital they had risked in backing an invention of which many of them could have had no first-hand knowledge; and made in the interest of a trade which was indeed a 'mystery' to them. Moreover, any new managing director would be loath to seek a quarrel with the manager of the factory in which the machines were made and the matrices cut. The natural and good-tempered strife that underlies the relations between the branch and the head office is always given a turn when authority changes hands and a new managing director takes charge.

Duncan's successor was William Isaac Burch, who had deputized for him on many occasions. He was a man of outstanding force and suppleness of character, closely in touch with the printing trade; and had long enjoyed the confidence of its leaders. A close business friend and ally was Walter Lewis, at that time manager of the Cloister Press at Heaton Mersey and about to become, in 1923, University Printer at Cambridge. Burch had more than once discussed with him the matter of new type-faces, and he was prepared to listen to Lewis's argument that the plan agreed to by his predecessor was a practical one and not merely 'idealist'. Accordingly the position of typographical adviser to the Corporation was then confirmed and the holder given an office at the headquarters. He was, however, in no position of power over the Monotype works. Burch found it convenient, in his own relations with the works, to be less imperative than his predecessor; all the more as the head of the works, F. H. Pierpont, a forceful character indeed, strongly opposed to 'interference' from the head office, was, too, a notorious upholder of the sovereignty of staff engineers, of practical accomplishments and of accepted values. The ideas of outside experts with theoretical learning but of unproved utility were and always would be resisted. By the engineers such theorists, like the customers who were regarded as a necessary evil, would be kept in their place. And to the factory heads, as to many of the sales staff, a typographical adviser had no place at all. The custom of cutting faces in response to, not in anticipation of, trade demands was, in 'works' and 'sales' opinion, not only the older but the wiser course. Accordingly the continuity of the plan hinged upon the possibility of counteracting the obstruction of the works by ensuring orders in advance for the matrices that were planned. It was, therefore, peculiarly fortunate that the typographical adviser to the Corporation should become associated in a similar capacity with the Cambridge Press, headed as it was by a Printer empowered to include or to exclude any typographical equipment that might be rendered available.*

Indications of a new step forward are to be seen in the Corporation's occasional publication *The Monotype Recorder*. The issue for January 1924 was printed at Cambridge in a revival of the roman type used for the *Hypnerotomachia Poliphili* which Aldus published in Venice in 1499, as described below. There were also designed, written and printed at Cambridge a number of broadsides and other publicity items, the like of which had not hitherto been seen in the trade. This was the beginning of the new educational kind of publicity, the principle of which Duncan had accepted and the sign of a move to create a modern advertising department, an unprecedented step, in this country at least. The new specimens were designed with some sense of style; they were necessarily full of history; the 'new' types were revivals of old ones.

When these designs were recut in the period 1922–32 there was no intention to encourage imitative typography, and none was installed at Cambridge with that end in view. There is no need, of course, to apologize for the use of typographical 'period' allusiveness in the right place. Presses faced with the task of presenting new editions of standard texts of historic importance at times find it necessary to reproduce old spellings and old alphabetical usages, as for example the long ſ and old ornaments. It is then a convenience to the press as well as a source of pleasure to readers to dress the edition with a period type, with contemporary head-pieces, tail-pieces and other ornaments that evoke the spirit of the time. But this sort of work is exceptional. The faces here described were brought to Cambridge to serve the general purposes of the Press. It happened, for reasons that then seemed good, that the programme, so far as it concerned the book-types in which the Press took a special interest, began with revivals. It is part of the purpose of this account to inquire how far the reasoning followed at that time seems good today.

In the first place, the general remark may be repeated that, as will be set forth in the following sections, the recutting of historic designs connoted from the beginning neither a hankering after the ancient as such, nor any prejudice against the modern or contemporary. The new Monotype programme was not drafted in strict accord with the underlying doctrine of a Morris, for whom return to the calligraphic standards of the pre-capitalist, and typographical models of the pre-industrial, ages would have seemed a paramount obligation. Nor had there been any superstitious regard for the work of 'contemporary' artists as such, and no slavish obedience to current 'trends' towards this or that 'modern' solution of the lettering 'problem'. The new programme was not romantic in either direction. It looked neither forward nor backward. The fact was that there were on the pages of books printed in the long and recent past several magnificent founts, engraved in periods when the art flourished, which had no present-day equivalent in point of nobility or utility, and had been rendered unobtainable by the effects of the great changes in taste and technique that swept over typography, as so much else, after the eighteenth century.

After the war the output of Germany continued to show more liveliness than that of any other country. Frankfurt rapidly regained the position of the greatest centre of typefounding in Europe that it possessed in the sixteenth and seventeenth centuries. This position was achieved on the basis of display types, i.e. designs intended for hand composition, above all for advertisements of every kind. Meanwhile machine composition strengthened its position in Germany as elsewhere. It became plain that something like the conservatism that already ruled newspaper composition would prevail in the making of books and periodicals. Twentieth-century writers such as Shaw and Wells would be presented in the dress of Dr Johnson and Alfred, Lord Tennyson. This came to pass. The problem of providing a new twentieth-century design for the composition of books by machine would await solution. Whether this solution would be found in Germany or Britain or America was by no means clear.

It was theoretically possible in England after 1922 to follow the example given by Germany since 1900. A school of contemporary designers could be created if they were given commissions by interested commercial firms. It was necessary, however, for the firms to know what instructions to give the artists. If the Germans had not succeeded in creating new book-types of permanent value, who else could? The roman design of which the trade in Germany continued to make the greatest use, apart from the native 𝔉raktur, was the modernization of Caslon which Miller & Richard of Edinburgh brought out in 1860. For all their great activity the Germans had made small progress along this line. What was the position in England?

The cutting for the Monotype of the Imprint face in 1912 was the one encouraging sign that had come from the trade. All the rest was so much duplication of the 1860 'old style' and the earlier 'modern'. Imprint was the first sign of contact between the Monotype and the trade—as it had now become—and the remnants of the craft as it had once been. The face was cut in 1912 at the prayer of the new generation of the Arts and Crafts Movement, then led by Lethaby, himself an admirer of the analogous German movement and protagonist for the application of sound design to utilitarian objects. The 1914–18 war upset the plans of the Lethaby generation.

There was every justification, therefore, in 1922 for an attempt to take farther the lead given in 1912 to the Monotype by Gerard Meynell and his associates. And this was all that the appointment of a typographical adviser to the Corporation amounted to: a new, or repeated, application of the Lethaby doctrine. But that doctrine did not demand reversion to antiquity and nothing else besides.

Yet at the time of decision, to revive historic designs was the only possible beginning. Such a decision did not necessarily involve following Morris and going to Venice, though it did render absolute obedience to his contention that 'whatever the subject-matter of the book may be, and however bare it may be of decoration, it can still be a work of art if the type be good and attention be paid to its general arrangement'; and to the corollary that 'legibility depends much on the design of the letter'. The return 'ad fontes' did not mean that the new Monotype programme must be initiated with one more Jensonian roman. What it did mean was that there were post-Jenson romans and italics worthy of emulation, and that it would be necessary to pass through this stage before anything like a stable 'twentieth-century' design could be within reach.

Years after the programme had been laid down a statement made by Bruce Rogers in America to a correspondent was made public which expresses the situation as it then existed so precisely that it may not be passed over at this point. The reader has been reminded above that Bruce Rogers had reported in 1917 upon the inadequacy of the Monotype repertory at Cambridge and had recommended additions. Writing in 1923 and echoing, in the first sentence here extracted, the judgement of Morris and of Walker, he reminded his correspondent 'As you know, however, I am not a great enthusiast over Caslon. It is at most a safe type for general use and moderately picturesque; but', he proceeded, 'there are so many other old models that are nobler in proportion and finer in drawing that it seems a pity one or more of them are not reproduced with the same fidelity that has been devoted to the Caslon and the Scotch.' Although the adverse criticisms of Walker and Morris, made in 1888 and 1893, will not be agreed to by some, none can deny that some pre-Caslon types are 'nobler in proportion and finer in drawing'. In fact the statement is a platitude to anybody who has taken the trouble, as Walker, Morris and Rogers had, to examine with care the types of the principal presses at work before and since Jenson. It is, in fact, so elementary a truth that the organizer of the Corporation's new programme deserves no credit for having come, independently, to the same conclusion as Bruce Rogers, and for having sought out those faces he believed to be noble in proportion and fine in drawing.

There were, then, solid reasons for choosing, out of the long and recent past, types that were 'noble' in proportion and 'fine' in drawing, as a first instalment of a new typographical programme; the whole without prejudice to the ultimate creation of designs, not immediately derived from the fine models of the past, yet fitted to enter into what Morris would recognize as works of art because they comprised good type, good arrangement and good paper. The original twentieth-century book type might come in due course. But certain lessons had first to be learnt and much necessary knowledge discovered or recovered. The way to learn to go forward was to make a step backward. These were the convictions with which the Monotype Corporation's new programme was drafted in January 1922, twenty-five years after the invention of the machine and after the British syndicate had begun business with a nondescript 'modern' face, copied without acknowledgement or payment to one of the typefounders.

The illustrations which follow are limited to types cut for the composition of books. As the later stage of the Monotype programme provided display types, it should be borne in mind that the account given of the Corporation's activities at this time is by no means complete. It may or may not be worth while to chronicle and describe the original designs cut or recut by the Corporation at the same time, which are now part of the routine of ephemeral typography in many countries. The designs here shown are those cut for the composition of scientific and general literature as distinct from advertising and commercial matter. To be precise, the pages that follow illustrate and describe ten types cut for trade use during the period 1922 to 1932. Seven are revivals of fifteenth to eighteenth-century originals. They are arranged in chronological order. Three are contemporary designs. They appear in their due position at the end of this 'tally'.

The following pages comprise, therefore, the revivals of those historic designs created by craftsmen at work during the Italian Renaissance (Centaur, Bembo, Polifilo, Blado), the French Renaissance (Garamond, Granjon) and the eighteenth century (Fournier le jeune, Baskerville, Bell). Later there was cut and installed at Cambridge a number of twentieth-century designs (Goudy Modern, Perpetua, and Times New Roman). It is proposed to take the faces in the order given above, although this is not the order in which they were cut or acquired. For the assistance of the reader the comment on the respective faces is composed in the type to which reference is being made, and displayed in accordance with the conventions of its period.

An appendix relates to three other types produced by the Monotype Corporation in the inter-war years but not used at Cambridge during the period 1922–32 with which this study was originally concerned. They are Van Dijck, Ehrhardt and Romulus.

CENTAUR ROMAN DESIGNED BY BRUCE ROGERS, BASED ON THE ORIGINAL OF NICOLAUS JENSON, VENICE 1470; CUT IN 1914 FOR COMPOSITION BY HAND AND IN 1929 FOR MONOTYPE COMPOSITION

To which is added the Arrighi italic of Frederic Warde based on the original print of Ludovico degli Arrighi, Rome, 1524. Cut for hand composition in 1925, and for machine composition, 1929.

N the period here under consideration, the most ancient and most classic of all the designs cut for mechanical composition is the Centaur of Bruce Rogers. The face was first cut privately for hand composition in 1914, and its recutting for Monotype composition necessarily, as it was private property, lay outside the programme adopted by the Corporation in 1922. Rogers's offer of the composing machine rights was made seven years later. This was a recognition of the success that had attended the revival of the Garamond and Polifilo romans with their respective italics, described in the pages which follow.

In the considered opinion of contemporary connoisseurs such as Emery Walker, Cobden-Sanderson and Newdigate, as well as of Rogers himself and Morris before them all, the roman used by Nicolaus Jenson for his *Eusebius* of 1470 is the most beautiful of all the letters of the fifteenth century. 'Jenson carried the development of roman type as far as it can go', said Morris. It was one of the sources of his own Golden type, which was destined fifty years later to find a home in Cambridge. But Morris decided against the delicacy of Jenson's drawing and preferred the distinctly darker version of the design used by another Venetian, Jacobus de Rubeis. It is a preference easier in his case to explain than to champion. Jenson's true model was later taken as the direct basis of the type of the Doves Bible, for which the Syndics of the Cambridge University Press acted as publisher in 1903–5.

The new Jensonian of Bruce Rogers differed notably from the previous recuttings. Rogers's version was a freehand emphasis of the calligraphic basis of the original. The re-drawing moved away from the original and there was produced, finally, a type that tended in some respects to be an independent design. It thus became the opposite of what Morris hated so much; an academically correct, pedantically accurate but dull and lifeless copy. Rogers's Centaur has a life of its own and a strong parental likeness to Jenson's roman. It retained the original proportions and, like the Golden and Doves types, bore itself with an aristocratic air which made it apt for the production of non-commercial editions, such as *Fra Luca de Pacioli* composed on the Monotype and printed at Cambridge in 1933 under Rogers's direction for the Grolier Club of New York. The great folio Oxford Bible in 1238 pages, mechanically composed in 22-point Centaur, provides the most monumental impression ever given to a Monotype face. The Oxford Bible compares only with two others; Estienne's folio Vulgate of four centuries earlier, composed in a 'gros texte' of Claude Garamond, and Baskerville's folio Authorized Version printed at Cambridge in 1763.

Baskerville knew what Garamond could hardly have foreseen: that roman and italic were to be ranked as inseparable companions on the printed page and in the one line. Jenson worked thirty years before italic appeared in print. And so Morris, Walker, Cobden-Sanderson and the other followers of Jenson were at a loss, with no guidance in this respect from him or any other printer of the fifteenth century. Rogers, however, did not ignore the problem in 1929 as he had in 1914. He adapted the model of Arrighi.

The italic made for Centaur is of later inspiration than the roman by fifty years. The original follows the first italic ever cut by an interval of twenty years. It is a rendering, as free and as calligraphic as Rogers's roman, of one of the finest of that category of italic nowadays called 'chancery cursives'. The first of these to be revived for trade use had been made for combination with the Polifilo roman (see p. 57 below). The acceptance by Rogers and others of the Roman, instead of the Venetian, type of cursive as the basis for the italics of Centaur (and Bembo and Polifilo) is one of the more significant factors in the 1922–32 period.

At this point it is appropriate to say that the italic used with Centaur is a version of one used in 1524 by Ludovico degli Arrighi from Vicenza, who practised in Rome. His types were from the hand of 'the great Lautizio', as Cellini styles him. The massive study by James Wardrop admirably illustrates the importance and versatility of this calligrapher and printer. The Monotype version was cut from the drawings made by Frederic Warde at the request of Bruce Rogers. As Rogers claimed at the completion of the first size, the Arrighi italic (here shown) is 'one of the finest and most legible cursive letters ever produced'. While a crisp piece of draughtsmanship, it preserves and even emphasizes its scriptorial origins, thus fitting it for companion use with such a calligraphic roman as Centaur, whose lower case so conspicuously reveals the use of the pen. In the Monotype cutting the capitals are inclined, whereas in the original the capitals are upright, as the convention required before the middle of the sixteenth century. The slightness and evenness of the angle of inclination of the chancery cursives make easy and comfortable their reading by the page, as may be seen in the Translator's Note appended to (T. E. Lawrence's) 'The Odyssey of Homer' which was composed at Cambridge for printing in London under the imprint of 'Emery Walker, Wilfred Merton and Bruce Rogers' in 1932.

The neo-Jenson and the neo-Arrighi combine to produce a result unattainable by the use of any other set of types. That result, it has been said, is 'aristocratic'. It is not in the least archaic. Morris was apt to say that one of the reasons for his exaltation of Jenson's roman above all others was that its creation lay outside all commercial considerations. So, too, Centaur makes no concessions to the exigencies of the contemporary publishing trade. But Bruce Rogers made one vital 'concession' to contemporary sense, as against the academic adhesion to the original to be seen in the Golden and Doves types. Both these formalize Jenson's solid horizontal and unbracketed serifs, which, in fact, are characteristic of all Venetian romans until the coming of Aldus. That is to say, for over a quarter of a century after the foundation of the first presses at Subiaco (Konrad Sweynheym and Arnold Pannartz, 1465) and Venice (Johann von Speyer, 1469), printers had either chosen, or been forced, to cut heavy, unbracketed, and in many cases blunt serifs to their faces. Could they not cut and cast fine bracketed serifs?

The question did not arise in the composition of liturgical and legal books in *textura* or even in *fere-humanistica*. But the cutting of fine serifs for sizes of type serviceable in literary and archaeological books was bound to arise when humanists like Felix Felicianus set about noting inscriptions and making careful copies of the old roman capitals. Also, the calligraphers of Florence and Naples were competing with printers and were expert with serifs by 1470; the style was spreading and bound to dominate before long. That Johann von Speyer and other printers at Venice should cut their relatively blunt serifs, may have been due to a sort of provinciality; or was it lack of the right tools or techniques?

We know little of the history of metals in the fifteenth century, but it seems possible that the Venetian printers,

like their colleagues then and since, had their casting difficulties. How else can the short life of punches and matrices
be explained? The probability is that the serif characteristic
of the Venetian romans before Aldus was technically pre-
destined. Either punchcutters before Francesco Griffo of
Bologna were unable to engrave with sufficient fineness; or,
alternatively, the striking of matrices from punches with
fine serifs was found too expensive of breakages. These are
the possibilities. Doubtless Sweynheym and Pannartz and
Johann von Speyer possessed the necessary steel, brass, copper,
tin and lead for the substance of their punches, matrices,
moulds and types. But neither they nor their generation
knew antimony. In consequence, all their metals, their steel
punches, copper matrices and lead types, were soft in comparison with later tools, the date of which can only be
guessed but could hardly have been before the very end of
the fifteenth century.

Documentation on the gradual introduction of hardening
processes in the metal trades has hardly begun, though Dr
Albert Giesecke made a welcome contribution to it a few
years ago. What is certain is that twenty years after the completion of Jenson's best roman, serifs were becoming finer.
There are many traces in books printed c. 1470 of efforts to
secure fine serifs. And of these traces Rogers has made the
most in his Centaur—thereby translating a fifteenth-century
roman of Jensonian proportions into sixteenth-century terms,
at the same time conferring upon it a note of the 'picturesque'
(the word is Rogers's used in a general connection) that the
Doves type lacks.

THE FIRST ROMAN USED BY ALDUS
MANUTIUS SHOWN IN THE DIALOGUE
'DE AETNA' BY PIETRO BEMBO, VEN-
ICE 1495. FIRST RECUT IN 1929 BY THE
MONOTYPE CORPORATION

*To which is added a cutting of an italic designed by Alfred
Fairbank and another italic, made standard for the fount,
originally designed by Giovantonio Tagliente, Venice 1524.*

Of the several romans used by Aldus the most noble
is the roman whose trade name is Bembo. It arrives
in order of historic precedence next to the roman of
Jenson, which is separated from it by an interval of
twenty-five years. Neither the Bembo roman nor the
press for which it was cut enjoys anything like the
praise given to the *Eusebius* roman and the press of
Nicolas Jenson. Few indeed have found anything to
admire in the romans (save one) of Aldus Manutius,
and everybody has condemned his greeks. According
to Morris, the types of 'the famous family of Aldus'
were 'artistically on a much lower level than Jenson's,
and in fact they must be considered to have ended the
age of fine printing in Italy'. Updike was less severe,
and prepared to admit one of the Aldine romans as

'excellent'. In his first edition (1922, p. 76) he had this to say of Aldus: 'His first roman letter, in which Bembo's *Aetna* [of 1495] appeared, was not particularly successful, but the third roman fount, designed by the celebrated Francesco Raibolini of Bologna [Griffo] who afterwards cut the Aldine italic character, was excellent. This roman type was used in that famous book, Colonna's *Hypnero-tomachia Poliphili* [of 1499] or "The Strife of Love in a Dream" printed by Aldus in the last year of the century.' Updike's second edition (1937) retains this passage, but there occurs in his valuable 'Supplementary Notes' (p. 280) a statement to the effect that further considera-tion led him to revise his opinion. '...I am inclined to give a little less credit to Jenson's types and more to the roman type used by Aldus in the *Hypnerotomachia* [of 1499] than formerly.' What had happened in the mean-time was that the roman thus approved had been recut by the Corporation. The circumstances are related in the next entry.

It was unfortunate that at the time the Corporation reproduced the roman of 1499 there existed no critical appreciation of Aldus's typographical merits. Nor has any such work been published since. It may safely be said that the opinion expressed by the latest writer is that of most living connoisseurs and bibliographers: 'Aldus was not a great printer in the sense that Nicolaus Jenson or Erhard Ratdolt, or even his own father-in · law Torresano, were masters of the art and technique of book-making. His presswork was indifferent and his types were poor. It has been said—I believe, with all possible justification—that his Greek types set back the study of that tongue by three hundred years. His type-cutter, Francesco Griffo of Bologna, has been described too enthusiastically as "one of the leading designers in typographical history".' This is the judgement of Dr Curt Bühler, a learned curator at the Pierpont Morgan Library, New York, passed on the occasion of the 500th anniversary of the birth of Aldus. This is not the place in which to suggest extenuations, as that by 1495 trade conditions had altered for the worse, or that Aldus's Greek could be no different from any other western Greek written with a western pen held in the western fashion, or that Griffo's roman dominated the trade from the end of the fifteenth to the middle of the seventeenth century. But one may be permitted to emphasize the point that the Aldine roman of 1495 had been in constant use since 1934 at the University Press of Yale, at which University Dr Bühler delivered his address in 1949. This is the roman now in the eye of the beholder. It was originally cut by Francesco Griffo, admired in Paris, with the roman of 1499, twenty years later by Simon de Colines and Robert Estienne, and copied at their instance by Augereau and Garamond. It is hard to believe that the two greatest printers of the French renaissance should each have followed Aldus out of sheer ignorance or superstition, or that they were unable to recognize 'poor' types when they saw them.

Modern disinclination to admit Aldus's romans into the decent company of Jenson and others is due, possibly, to the lack of critical material or, what is the same thing, to dependence upon insufficient or bad facsimiles. There did not exist in Morris's time any great collection of facsimiles. Much has been done to remedy this and, as we all know, an immense amount of work has been accomplished under the impulse of Robert Proctor. Even so, for reasons of space, Bembo's *Aetna* is given only a dozen lines of facsimile in the most authoritative and accessible source: the B.M. *Catalogue of Books printed in the XVth Century* (Part V, 1924). Konrad Burger's *Monumenta Germaniae et Italiae Typographica* (Berlin, 1913), which is a fine and full collection of facsimiles, was the staple of Updike's knowledge of fifteenth-century books. Few would have said at the time that it did not present the best available corpus of specimens of the period. It does not contain a single exhibit from the Aldine press.

The principal fact about the *Aetna* is that the virtues of the book as a book, and of the type as a design, can only be appreciated if more than one page, and preferably the whole, of Bembo's tract is studied and compared with other work of Aldus's own office and that of other printers. As far as the Bembo tract is concerned it is well if several copies can be studied together, and seen with Aldus's other productions in roman. If this is done it will appear that, letter for letter, Aldus's third roman is no advance on his first: that the type of the *Hypnerotomachia Poliphili* of 1499 is in certain respects inferior to that of the *Aetna* of 1495. In particular the capitals of the *Aetna* are better related to the lower case. The two alphabets in the *Aetna* blend harmoniously to a perfect degree, whereas in the *Polifilo* the capitals take on a quasi-independent status. Notwithstanding, it is obvious that the types of both the *Aetna* and the *Polifilo* are varieties of the same design. It was destined to have a lasting effect on the trade. Garamond and Granjon accepted it as their prototype; it was their romans, absolutely faithful to the Aldine, that set the style for Van Dijck, and were set by him for Caslon.*

Its uninterrupted career of nearly three centuries confers upon it a look of familiarity which makes it less archaic than any pre-Aldine Venetian face. It was inspired not by writing but by engraving; not script but sculpture. It rendered all preceding romans archaic. There is one roman only that prefigures somewhat the type of the *Aetna*: that used at Lyon in 1493 (the punches were probably cut in Italy) by Johann Trechsel.

In the pages of *De Aetna* the type, then new, looks almost as fresh as if it had come off a present-day type-caster. Manifestly it did come from the hand of a uniquely competent engraver who, perhaps because Aldus had access to some hardening element, encouraged the cutting of serifs finer than had been the custom. The lower case is more brilliant than any of its predecessors, and the design as a whole ranks with the roman of Louis XIV (which brought to a close the two-hundred-year reign of the *Aetna* type) as one of the major typographical 'watersheds'. This is obvious today, but it was not until 1924 that the typographical adviser of the Monotype Corporation became aware of the fact, i.e. after the type of the *Polifilo* had been recut.

The superior proportions and clarity of the *Aetna* type as recut, in comparison with that of the *Polifilo*, need no description. They are on exhibition in these pages. There is, moreover, no point in repeating what has been said about the merits of the design and its later career in the introduction to W. Turner Berry and A. F. Johnson, *Catalogue of Specimens of Printing Types by English and Scottish Printers and Founders, 1665–1830*. The justification of the Monotype reproduction is its appearance on the page. It remains regrettable that the knowledge available in 1923 was insufficient, and that, in consequence, we have two contemporary faces of closely similar design. In the course of time Polifilo will become obsolete. The proof lies in the wider use made of Bembo at home, on the continent, and in the U.S.A. It is pleasant to be able to add that fine use is being made of it in Italy.

But although the obsolescence of the Polifilo roman may be safely predicted, it is unlikely that a similar fate awaits the Blado italic cut to accompany it. As this italic may well outlive the roman, it is accorded separate entry (pp. 57 ff.). Discussion of the problem of italic is better deferred to the next entry, but it must be acknowledged now that, despite the success of the Blado italic in 1923, much hesitation was felt when question of the italic for Bembo required settlement in 1928.

The first endeavour was to create a new chancery cursive based upon the hand of the most accomplished living English scribe available for the purpose, Alfred Fairbank. This italic was duly commissioned and cut. It appears before the reader in the present paragraph. It had the great virtue of all the chancery cursives: it was legible in mass and can easily be read by the page. So much so that, in fact, it looked happier alone than in association with the Bembo roman. Owing to insufficient knowledge or faulty analysis, the problem may have been insoluble along the lines attempted, for it was seen that when used in close association with the roman, i.e. in the same line, the capitals of this chancery cursive appeared independent and inharmonious, and the lower case constricted and unassimilable.* The design, finely conceived and remarkably well drawn, looked its best when given sole possession of the page. The statement may be verified if the quarto edition of Robert Bridges's 'The Testament of Beauty' (Oxford, 1929) is referred to. This was one of the first uses of the Bembo roman, and Fairbank's italic, when first seen, appeared so well by itself that Bridges wished, at an early stage, to set the whole of his poem in it. Finally, the Bembo roman was chosen but the two-page 'Note on the Text' is wholly composed in the italic lower case combined with roman capitals, and it is used throughout the 'Testament' for emphasis and quotation. The test led to a decision to allow this italic the chance of a separate career.

The following paragraph is set in the standard italic cut to accompany the Bembo roman, based on an original print of Giovantonio Tagliente, Venice, 1524.

An italic for Bembo having less personality was searched for, and found in the publication of the writing-master, Giovantonio Tagliente, practising in Venice from 1524. The face used for the text of this writer's early compilations is a fine flowing chancery cursive with an abundance of ligatures and swashes. It must have been difficult to cut and to cast, for it had the short life of three years. For the use intended to be made of it in 1929 it had to be severely revised. The ascenders were serifed, and the roman capitals mechanically slanted. On the whole it has to be said that while the first italic has too much personality the second has too little. While not disagreeable, it is insipid; though it may serve the Bembo roman in some slavish sort its absence of character unfits it for textual use. The italic for Bembo cannot be accused of being a specimen of what Morris so much hated in architectural revivalism: pedantry. Rather the Bembo italic is a vulgarization. In this respect the Blado italic is a much superior achievement. But both the chancery cursive for Centaur and for Bembo were cut more than a quarter of a century later than the respective romans they are made to accompany.

In justice to Tagliente and his unnamed punchcutter it should be emphasized that the italic shown in the immediately preceding lines does little more than adapt the forms of the original, a reproduction of which appears in an article on italic contributed to the second volume of *The Fleuron*. A critical and definitive account of the early history of italic will not fail to praise Tagliente's original. It is in the highest degree probable that the punches were cut after a design by the master himself.

THE THIRD ROMAN USED BY ALDUS
MANUTIUS AND FIRST SHOWN IN
THE HYPNEROTOMACHIA POLIPHILI
VENICE 1499. FIRST RECUT IN 1923
BY THE MONOTYPE CORPORATION

To which is added a recutting of the fourth italic of Ludovico Arrighi,
originally used for the 'Apologia of Petro Collenucio', Rome 1526.

ATIN was not the abiding love of Teobaldo Manucci, better known as Aldo Manuzio or Aldus Manutius. He early became a devotee of Greek, talked Greek in his household, staffed his office with Greeks and printed his first book in Greek. Latin letters came next and the tract (see pp. 46 ff.) by the future Cardinal Bembo was his first contribution to typography in that language. The *Hypnerotomachia Poliphili* was published in 1499, when Aldus was in his fiftieth year. He was to live to the age of sixty-five but never to produce a finer work. It is the book, indeed, upon which his fame as a printer rests. The reputation of the work derives, however, from the marvellous quality of the illustrations, their drawing and engraving on wood; and the superbly harmonious effect of their association with the type on the printed page, set as the book is, to the most agreeable dimensions, with a line of exactly the right length for the size of the type and the comfort of the reader. But the type itself has never been very highly esteemed.

The idea of reproducing the type came from Harry Lawrence, formerly of the firm of Lawrence and Bullen. The firm had published a number of English translations of

Italian renaissance novels, etc. Bullen later left to publish Elizabethan studies at the Shakespeare Head Press, which he founded for the purpose at Stratford-on-Avon, and Lawrence associated himself with the Medici Society, a London publishing house. In 1923 Lawrence was projecting a translation of the whole, or a portion, of the *Dream of Polifilo*, printing it in type-facsimile and, of course, reproducing the illustrations. The project was ultimately abandoned; but the type was proceeded with. It was recreated, as it stood, from sheets of the original that were supplied by Lawrence, who had them from an imperfect copy. The printed letters were one by one reproduced with their outlines as impressed on the paper. The result is what Morris would have called a 'pedantic' piece of work; and so, with slight qualification, it is. It was possible, in fact, to compose, according to the correct dimensions of the original, a page of the Monotype version, place it side by side with the original, and find no difference except in paper. This test was in fact made, and, naturally, it gave the greatest satisfaction to the works. Everybody was amazed and gratified at this demonstration of what could be achieved by conscientious photography, exact tracing and efficient engraving. It was no longer to be doubted that the technical resources available guaranteed a reproduction, faithful to the point of pedantry, of an original, the revival of which had never before been attempted. Unlike Garamond's roman (see below) no typefounder had recut Aldus's. The Polifilo roman was, therefore, a contribution. Whether a new and vital design could eventually be created by these means only was another matter, and one that will be discussed later. To redraw, and not merely reproduce, an ancient original, available only in the form of a contemporary print, was a more difficult art than direct imitation; and this was what Rogers had accomplished with his

Centaur. But the Corporation had not in 1923 the experience gained later. Centaur was six years ahead and, even so, had first been cut by a craftsman for hand composition.

It must be conceded, therefore, that the Polifilo, as recut for mechanical composition in 16-point in 1923, was a technical achievement of some value. It was also an instant success; and still, thirty years later, finds abundant recognition at home and abroad in the small, as well as large, sizes. Cambridge acquired it early and employed the 16-point for the text of *Four Centuries of Fine Printing*, printed for Ernest Benn, Ltd in 1924. As the project of a type-facsimile of the *Dream of Polifilo* had been abandoned, this became the first modern use of any of Aldus's types; and no fair judge could, or can, doubt that the roman makes a very handsome appearance on the broad page of this book.

It cannot be claimed, however, that the Monotype recutting is perfect in point of reproduction technique. It is accurate without realizing the intention of the original. What came out in Venice in 1499 is a brilliant piece of work, which deserves much higher praise than it has received. The five, six and in some places seven, lines of capitals serving as headings to the *libri* into which the text is divided are composed magnificently in the capitals of the body fount. They exhibit to the full the deliberate inscriptional quality of the design and emphasize it by the use of the spread M, long-tailed Q and R. It is the more deplorable, therefore, that the complete beauty of the composition should be marred by Aldus's blameworthy, because avoidable, carelessness in alignment and spacing. It is much to be regretted, too, that due care was not taken in 1923 to find the best pages for the reconstruction and the reproduction of the fount instead of relying upon the sheets provided by Lawrence. The original 1499 edition varies notably from page to page. Some sections of the book are printed from sparkling new, others from soft and old, type. Unfortunately the leaves presented to the Corporation by Lawrence were detached from the less well-printed portions. In the result, the recutting lacks the grace of the type as it appeared in its earliest casting. At the time the typographical adviser's knowledge was insufficient and it was not thought necessary to compare the recorded copies; the work was considered pressing; the leaves were at hand.

The error was grave though not catastrophic, as the text of *Four Centuries* demonstrates. The line of those pages is long, but in the mass the type bears very pleasantly the slight wear and extra weight that the Monotype works reproduced from the impressions on the original leaves which they had received. The 'worn' effect would naturally appear to the maximum in large sizes and no lower case above 16-point has been cut. In the smaller sizes the 'worn' effect disappears, and the design may be said to look its best in 12-point. Certain capitals are complete failures. Owing to the degree of misapplied care taken to ensure conformity with the original the alignment is uneven at both head and foot. Everything taken into account, the recutting of the Polifilo roman must be judged as a moderate success only, redeemed by the cutting of Bembo.

੯ੈ THE REVIVED CHANCERY ITALIC
OF ARRIGHI ੭ु

ORIGINALLY USED FOR PETRUS COLLENUCIUS
'APOLOGI'
PRINTED BY LUDOVICO ARRIGHI
ROME 1526
RECUT BY THE
MONOTYPE CORPORATION 1923

The category of italic here seen, to which that cut for Bembo also belongs, is now well understood and is even fashionable. In 1923 its character and virtue were known to few beyond Robert Bridges, Edward Johnston and Alfred Fairbank.* It began as a special script reserved for the execution of a distinct, and relatively recent, class of diplomatic document, the Brief, expedited by the most exalted chancery in the world—that of the Roman Curia. The Brief began its formal existence some time before 1390, and then in gothic cursive. It so continued for a generation. Precisely when this gothic gave way to the humanistic has not been found, though it doubtless will, by Monsignor Karl August Fink in the course of his researches into the early history of the papal Brief. But, it is safe to say, the change to humanistic occurred while Flavio Antonio Blondo and, secondly, Poggio Bracciolini headed the secretariat under Pope Eugenius IV. The earliest humanist Brief on record is dated 1446. The text is an upright semi-formal 'roman' and its signature is in upright cursive, 'Blondus', the scholar known to have been writing a humanistic cursive as early as 1422. Apparently, the adoption of this cursive for the text, and not merely for signatures of Briefs, came between the pontificates of Eugenius IV and Pius II.* Under the latter the Brief became larger in scale, as we know from one of the kind dated 1462 surviving at Basel. This is a well written piece of the slightly cursive

57

humanistic that, by then, had long become the common medium among scholars. As men like Pomponio Leto wrote it, the hand was small, fast and ligatured wherever possible. Thus, in the first quarter of the century, in Blondus's time, cursive humanistic served two purposes, the literary as well as the diplomatic. At the end of the century (in the time of Leto), the literary form of the humanistic cursive was fast and small, and the diplomatic form relatively formal and generous in size. In other words, the literary expression was less expensive of time and material than the diplomatic. This division became permanent; the literary form tended to become more minute and the diplomatic form larger. Generations hence were to find the former become smaller and plainer and the latter larger and decorated.

The typographic form was bound to follow the literary form, if only because it was minute, economic and familiar to scholars. Its first appearance in the printed page in 1500 reproduces the fast, minute and highly ligatured bookscript of the kind practised by Leto until he died in 1497. It is not at all remarkable that the economy in space of such a cursive should have led to the engraving of italic. What is remarkable is that it should not have been accomplished for Latin until 1500–1, when, in fact, it had been done for Greek by Aldus himself in 1495, though certainly on a much larger body. The ligatures required in both Greek and Latin cursive were very many. Their number argues that the cost of paper exceeded the cost of the labour of punchcutters and compositors—but it is to be remembered that Aldus's Greek was set up by Greeks.

The Aldine italic of 1500–1 was immediately copied in Venice and outside. It is singular, therefore, that not for the space of twenty years did anything of the kind appear in Rome, and, when it did, the Venetian literary form was abandoned in favour of a version or rather number of versions of the older diplomatic cursive. Some of these chancery cursive types kept their position over a number of years. The temptation to narrate their career here must be resisted.

It is required, however, to note in chronological order the modern faces of the kind cut or recut since Edward Johnston designed, as appears,

58

the first chancery cursive, for which Edward Prince and George Friend cut the punches. Johnston's chancery italic appeared in the colophon of the Cranach 'Virgil', published in 1926 at Weimar by Count Harry Kessler, but it was never seen in a page of text until Rilke's 'Duineser Elegien' appeared from the same Press in 1931. The Johnston fount was probably not designed for prose composition but, occasionally, for verse, and normally as a means of emphasis and distinction. It is a 'regular' chancery type, compact and angular, with ascenders which are unserifed and curve to the right, and descenders which curve to the left. It is not well aligned and some of the characters are roughly fitted. Though it has little beauty in itself it is of great interest as the first, and at least an independent, return to the model of the Roman chancery. In sum the idea of such an italic came to Johnston and Kessler about 1914 but the project was not realized until 1925.*

While Johnston's design, begun about 1914, unquestionably ranks as the pioneer of this category of italic the attendant circumstances obstructed its serving to inspire any successors. It received no publicity, and its existence, even as an experiment, was unknown in 1922. It was many years later during a conversation with Count Kessler that the present writer learnt of the design, and still later that G. T. Friend lent him Johnston's original drawings.

Hence the present italic has a completely independent history; yet it owes an indirect obligation to Johnston. It was fig. 180 in his 'Writing, Illuminating and Lettering' that was recognized by this writer as the most rational and speedy of all the current humanistic scripts and made to serve as model for his own hand. This was in 1913* when the writer first met Edward Johnston, a decade before the Monotype Corporation gave him the opportunity to revive the present italic.

This italic was the first revival in the trade, since Blado's time, of any 'chancery' italic. Like the Polifilo roman, it was reproduced direct from the printed page without redrawing or allowance for spread of ink. It has the great value of being even in colour with the roman. Acquired by the Press in 1924 and used in 'Four Centuries of Fine Printing', the Blado chancery italic thus appeared in print in 1924, a year before Edward Johnston's chancery italic appeared in the Cranach Virgil. The original of the Bembo italic was the third fount of Arrighi (see p. 43). It originated in Rome in 1526 but it was the 'Vita Sfortiae' of Paolo Giovo printed by Antonio Blado in 1539 that served as the basis for the recutting in 1923.*

The revival of the Roman chancery style and Arrighi's typographical expression of it, as typified in the present italic, cut, it has been seen, for Blado, may be ranked as a success. It needs to be added that the capitals of Blado are sloped, agreeably with the convention established by the French punchcutters whose work it is time to consider.

THE 'GARAMOND' ROMAN

CUT BY THE MONOTYPE CORPORATION IN 1922

IN the new programme of type-design adopted by the Monotype Corporation in 1922 a face of French renaissance origin was given first place. It was necessary in the early stages of the new Monotype effort, which included the Polifilo roman and Blado italic, to be satisfied that the works could produce accurate facsimiles of an antique printed original. That this was a required preliminary had been made clear by the failure of a previous attempt to produce a facsimile made from original types, i.e. series 128 'Caslon Old Face'. Although this series gave, and gives, satisfaction to the general trade, it is a complete failure as a facsimile. Of course, the making of a facsimile of anything, even with the best contemporary photographic methods, is not an easy matter. The task of exactly reproducing types is very difficult, and probably the time, 1916, is partly to blame for the deficiencies of series 128. But the originals in the instance of this series were types newly cast by the Caslon foundry and gave less trouble than is involved in the redrawing of an original, available only in the form of a print that may not be at all sharp. The task of renovating or recreating a design from old impressions is the most difficult of all. The effect of impressing upon damp paper, of worn type, and of the spread of ink, have to be reckoned with; and great skill is needed if, while removing blurred outlines, the subtleties of the original engraving are not to be lost.

The reproduction of the roman in series 156, now before the reader, was made from a contemporary print taken off the presses of the Imprimerie Nationale. It is, generally speaking and certainly in some sizes, successful. One or two points may be remarked now that the series has been in use for thirty years. These lines set in the 14-point of the roman show the design to the best advantage; but the smaller sizes, particularly 8-point roman, are very fine pieces of engraving, with valuable economic gains in comparison with similar sizes of dissimilar designs.

The design itself has been described above as originating during the French renaissance. The revival is not a new or unprecedented contribution to the trade as are Bembo and Polifilo and their italics, or Baskerville, etc. In the recutting of this design, as with Bodoni in 1921, the Monotype Corporation was anticipated by the American Type Founders Company of Jersey City. They brought out in 1918 a design called 'Garamond'. As an original 'old face' recut by an experienced foundry, the design had a crispness and, as it then appeared, a certain novelty of style lacking in Caslon.

In 1920 the Cloister Press of Heaton Mersey imported three sizes of Garamond for the hand-composing department. The first use made in Europe of the American 'Garamond' was for the text of *Catherine*, the epic by R. C. K. Ensor (London, Sidgwick and Jackson, 1921). The late Frank Sidgwick, who was a scholarly publisher and incidentally an old friend of Walter Lewis, was delighted to have the first use of the new type for Ensor's poem, and required a short historical note on the face to accompany the book. This note was not based upon any independent knowledge, but on the authorities available. And these, as will be seen below, were not at all points as authoritative as then appeared.

It was natural that the list of *desiderata* made for the benefit of the Monotype Corporation should seek to give Garamond a place with Aldus, Fournier, Baskerville and others. What was then thought to be Garamond's authentic roman was completed in one size (24-point) in 1922. An historical account of it was written for the benefit of the Corporation's publicity department. The same writer was responsible for a description of the type which appears in the 1923 *Penrose Annual*, when he dissertated about Garamond himself.

The attribution of the roman to Garamond, though not then regarded as above suspicion, was unchallengeable. The majesty and the allure of A. Claudin's *Histoire de l'Imprimerie en France* (Paris, 1900–14; four volumes), the erudition and authority of A. Christian, director of the Imprimerie Nationale, who inspired Claudin and printed his work ('probably', says Updike, 'the finest book on printing that has ever been published') silenced criticism. Moreover, Updike's acceptance of the attribution in *Printing Types*, the two volumes of which appeared in the autumn of 1922, gave it additional authority. Yet it remained that the 'Garamond' roman of the Imprimerie Nationale, which had been used as the basis of the American and the Monotype recutting, did not really look as if it came from the hand of any punchcutter working *c.* 1540, as Bernard, Duprat, and Christian believed. The matter demanded thorough investigation. In the meantime the ascription of the types to Garamond held the field.

It was not until the editor of *The Fleuron* secured the services of Paul Beaujon, then resident in Paris, that the facts necessary for placing the 'Garamond' roman of the Imprimerie Nationale in its proper context were assembled. The article in vol. v (Cambridge, 1926) proved that the ascription to Garamond of the roman and italic called 'Caractères de l'Université' in the old inventories of the Imprimerie Nationale could not be sustained. It was shown that these romans were in fact excellent copies of authentic Garamonds by the expert seventeenth-century punchcutter Jean Jannon (1580–1658). It was his ambition, Jannon says (in the specimen he published in 1621 which Paul Beaujon was the first to examine), to revive the glories of Robert Estienne at Paris, 'qui ont esté fort celebres en leur temps', Plantin at Antwerp, and Wechel at Frankfurt. All Jannon's heroes knew well the merits of incomparably the greatest of all the highly talented school of engravers of roman working in Paris during the first half of the sixteenth century—Claude Garamond, though Jannon does not mention him. Two generations had sufficed to render his name unknown outside a narrow circle in Paris. The main facts about him are as follows.

Claude Garamond (died 1561) was apprenticed about 1510 to Antoine Augereau (d. 1534) who had worked as punchcutter and founder for Simon de Colines, looked upon by some as the greatest printer of the greatest period of French book production. He certainly had more responsibility than any other man for the policy of abandoning gothic in favour of roman; and for setting up, as the model for Paris punchcutters, the romans of Aldus. By 1520 Garamond, out of his apprenticeship, was working with Geofroy Tory. From the year 1528 Colines, Tory, and Robert Estienne are found using a set of romans then new in Paris.*

Some of these came without doubt from Augereau and others from the hand of Garamond. In 1532 there appeared a book that ranks as the finest monument to the printing and typefounding skill of the time: the great folio Vulgate in 1172 pages, with apparatus and shoulder notes using Hebrew and Greek; the whole under the imprint set out in superb capitals of 'gros canon', slightly spaced between the letters: PARISIIS EXCVDEBAT ROBERTVS STEPHANVS IN SVA OFFICINA. ANN. M.D.XXXII. VIII. IDVS NOVEMB. These capitals can safely be ascribed to Garamond. At about this time he was working in association with Pierre Haultin,* a celebrated engraver of characters for the printing of music. For André Chevallon (and later his widow) Garamond cut several romans. Between 1540 and 1546 he cut the 'grecs du roy' for Robert Estienne, and numerous romans for his own account. With Pierre Gaultier as his printer, he began in 1545 the publication of books. On the advice of Jean de Gaigny, then Chancellor of the Sorbonne, and deeply interested in printing, he brought out, by himself or in partnership, at least five pocket texts of Juvencus, Lactantius and Thucydides and other editions of ancient authors. He also printed a piece by a contemporary, *Pia et Religiosa Meditatio* by David Chambellan, canon of Notre-Dame.

The typographical importance of this series of books is that they contain a quantity of italic cut on small bodies, in which, Garamond says in his Epistle to Chambellan, he endeavoured to approximate the model of Aldus. But Garamond did not slavishly copy the Aldine italic, and for his larger size, i.e. a cicero as used by Aldus, reduced the ligatures. Also he cut a second italic called by the trade 'glossa'. Features of it that will not be overlooked are the sloped capitals and the treatment of some of these as 'swash' characters. The device of sloping the capitals of the italic was new, or newish; it is one of the important differences that separate the italics of Aldus and Arrighi from those of Garamond, Colines and, it might be added, Janot.*

These being the saliencies about Garamond it is necessary to record that he was incomparably the finest engraver of romans among the great first generation of French renaissance printers and publishers who, with Geofroy Tory, Henri Estienne and his foreman and executor Simon de Colines, led the movement away from gothic and towards roman. Their patron and pattern was Aldus, deliberately chosen by Colines. The engravers who worked for Colines and Estienne were served with patterns selected with the same scrupulosity that was part of their scholarship. Augereau's and Garamond's romans were modelled closely and intelligently upon Aldus's. Every one of Garamond's romans is above praise and some have never been equalled.

These, then, were the romans which Jannon endeavoured eighty years after the death of Garamond to recreate. He was, in fact, for some years before 1621, occupied in an effort precisely similar to that being made by the Monotype Corporation in 1922: to imitate the typographical style, in its purity, of the great masters of the roman letter and to make available to the trade faces that had once been esteemed. The quality of Jannon's reproduction of his chosen romans is remarkable, but it cannot be said to yield anything like a close facsimile. The grace and suavity peculiar to Garamond are absent. Instead there is a crispness and hardness of line which evokes the spirit rather of Paris than of Geneva, whence Jannon came.* The Monotype reproduction of Jannon's roman is faithful and exact. That the name Garamond was given to the roman in 1922 is to be regretted, but the huge commercial success of the series is due to the merits of the design which, it has been established, is Garamond's though at a distinct remove. For reasons that appear in pp. 68–70 the italic of Jannon was not reproduced. A model artistically more agreeable and historically correct was chosen.

The Italic of Robert Granjon

ORIGINALLY CUT FOR THE PRINTER OF PARIS
1530

FIRST RECUT BY THE MONOTYPE CORPORATION
1922

URING the sixteenth century the Parisian cutters were in complete agreement with Simon de Colines and Robert Estienne that the romans of Aldus should be their standard. The situation in Paris regarding italic in comparison with roman was less unanimous and certain. It has been seen that the Aldine and Arrighian italics diverged in a principal point of function, and therefore of design. But fundamentally both were set on the same course: to serve as an alternative to roman as a text fount. The reservation of italic to such incidental uses as for extract and emphasis in a body of roman text never occurred to any Italian printer and only became a convention in France towards the end of the sixteenth century. In the first half of that century italic text is found sprinkled with the titles of books in roman; the reverse custom came later, and with it other subordinate uses of italic which have since become standard in roman typography, and so remain. Between 1525 and 1535 italic was in the process of breaking out of its calligraphic conventions. It could not then break out of them all, and it is difficult to see how it can do so today, though a determined effort has been made in recent years to drive out all traces of calligraphic parentage.

The designing of an italic which shall serve the text of books is not without its trouble. To make an italic that will align and harmonize when set with roman in the same line, paragraph and page is very difficult. Aldus had never attempted this problem; nor Arrighi. In modern times Morris and Cobden-Sanderson avoided it. But for them, as private practitioners, it could hardly have been an anxious matter, or even for Aldus and Arrighi since they were not engaged in printing for controversy. But Paris in the 1530's was, more than any other printing centre, the theatre of the fiercest and the most acrimonious political and theological faction.

Garamond came late to the consideration of the necessity to mix roman with italic and he represents a transition between Arrighi and Granjon, between the Rome of 1525 and the Lyon of 1550. The root question was the extent to which the italic should be assimilated to roman; or vice versa. The commercial success of Aldus, with his cheap classics which were copied wholesale in type and format by other publishers, was to some extent a menace to roman. From the economic point of view it is still difficult to understand why italic did not more seriously threaten roman. It was so much more compact than roman, took in so many more letters to the line, and could look equally well. Why is it found between 1501 and 1550 giving so much competition to roman as a text face and then by 1590 yielding so much as, ultimately, to be content to serve as an auxiliary face? The course of the rise and decline of italic in Italy and France is not known in detail. The *œuvre* of Granjon (whose work we have shortly to describe), if accurately distinguished, would illuminate this remote branch of typographical history.

Garamond's italics are of interest in this connection. His note to Chambellan suggests that he cut only two italics and had never cut any before 1545;* which is difficult to believe, but may be true. What is important is that, although he was not the first to flourish and slope the capitals of his italics, the example he gave as 'tailleur de caractères du roy' lent the practice authority. Whereas his great Italian near-contemporaries kept their italics under the discipline of roman capitals, Garamond (apparently after hesitation) joined the new fashion that had come into Paris from Lyon via Basel, c. 1537. He cut fewer ligatures (which had made the original Aldine letter difficult to imitate). Moreover, he multiplied the swashes which Aldus never used and which Arrighi invented and used occasionally as a decorative device. It is curious that, at the time when the calligraphic ancestry of italic was being ignored, a determination to decorate it should become manifest.

The structural means taken to accommodate the decoration (not that it was necessary) was to abandon the principle consecrated in Venice and Rome of upright capitals, and to adopt the Basel and Lyon fashion of sloping, swashing and displaying them, without respect whatsoever to calligraphic sense. In the title-pages of his own publications, Garamond uses inclined swashed capitals without any sign of the discretion shown by contemporary calligraphers and by Garamond's early patron, Colines. The latter's chancery italic, in use from 1530, having cursive terminals to ascenders and descenders, with upright capitals leavened with swashes, was never allowed the misuse noticeable in Parisian printing of the next decade. The vice is principally noticeable in books of small format. Skill and discretion were bestowed upon the quartos and folios of Gabriel Buon, Michel Vascosan and Fédéric Morel, whose larger books challenge comparison with the masterpieces of their fathers. Intelligent and stylish use was made of the new post-Colines italics in such sizes as 'gros romain' and 'petit paragon', the authorship of which is touched upon in a subsidiary paragraph. Some of these combined sloping capitals with a flowing lower case reminiscent, though not reproductive, of Arrighi's chancery italics in scale and style. The Paris italics ultimately penetrated the whole trade even as far as Rome; and, well before the end of the century, the standard italic of literary Europe was one that established its power so securely that it was not challenged for two centuries. While the learned world read a roman immediately dependent upon the Aldine model as shown in Bembo's *De Aetna* of 1495, the italic they read, as a subsidiary, was an independent development. This is one of the salient facts regarding roman and italic in the sixteenth century. It is necessary to add that, for reasons that will appear in the section of this book that deals with Eric Gill's Perpetua, italic, despite the efforts made in the sixteenth century and since, has successfully resisted complete deprivation of its calligraphic inheritance. It has been aided by the roman lower case, which also has a calligraphic ancestry that remains obvious enough in a, g, and in other characters.

But the pedigree of all the constituents of the single alphabet, roman or italic, capitals or lower case, is both mixed and complicated. The present-day printer's idea of his alphabetical equipment, expressed in terms of one root design, is a set of capitals, small capitals, lower case, italic capitals and italic lower case, with numerals, bold capitals and lower case, and the necessary ligatures, etc. This conception of an alphabetical equipment began in Paris about the middle of the sixteenth century when roman and italic were first seen (some time before 1590) as fellow halves of a single design.* This was one of the great technical (i.e. in terms of composition) advances. The assimilation of capitals with lower case, of majuscules with minuscules, established with such difficulty and delay between the sixth and the eighth centuries, is an analogy. The practical assimilation of roman and italic was exploited in the seventeenth century. The only 'bold' then was black-letter. Bold was not assimilated to roman and italic until the twentieth century. But the process began with Garamond and Granjon.*

Much labour needs to be spent upon the romans and italics of the period 1560–90, before the principal Paris and Lyon founts can be assigned with any confidence to the shops of Garamond, Granjon, Haultin and Le Bé I and II. Knowledge has been accumulated since 1922, when the Monotype Corporation initiated its programme. It became known in 1930 that the matrices of the pica italic comprised in the Fell donation to the University of Oxford are struck from the punches cut by Granjon; and it is hoped that the new *Specimen* now being prepared by the Printer to the University of Oxford will distinguish, more closely than was possible for his predecessor, the pedigrees of the several designs (roman, italic, greek and exotic) in that celebrated bequest.* For the present, it is enough to say that the work of one of the greatest of all punchcutters, comparable with Garamond himself, has been safeguarded in England, by the possession, since 1692, at the Oxford University Press, of this (and probably other) unique sets of original matrices. As will be seen from the following text, Granjon's Paris italic was highly ligatured. He was, without doubt, second only to Garamond in expertness and greater in versatility.

Robert Granjon, son of Jean of that name, also a printer and publisher in Paris, of whom one book is known to have been brought out (Paris, 1506), was active as a punchcutter and founder from about 1545. As Garamond knew, it was not the punchcutter, the founder, or even the printer, but the publisher who got the 'honey', as he told the Bishop of Soissons in 1545. In 1549 Granjon published under his own imprint 'Parisiis Apud Robertum Granjon, in taberna Gry-phiana' a pocket New Testament in Greek and Latin. By 1551 he was in partnership with Michel Faisandat (or Fezendat), and published that year the three octavos which are listed by Baudrier. While in Paris he furnished (strikes of) an italic to Jean de Tournes I (1504–64) of Lyon, where he was regularly seen from 1546, and where he married the daughter of Bernard Salomon, the fine wood-engraver, who was attached to Jean de Tournes. About 1556–7, Gran-jon established himself at Lyon, partly working as a punchcutter and founder for de Tournes and partly publishing (on his own account) books printed in the 'Civilité' (i.e. bastard Secretary) scriptorial types of his cutting, as well as books composed in the musical notation he had cut. This occupied Granjon until 1562, when he left Lyon for Paris, gave up publishing and returned to work as a founder. His relations with Christopher Plantin were close and long-sustained from 1565, but they did not prevent his selling strikes to printers in Italy and Switzerland, as well as France and the Netherlands. He may have been the first, or one of the first (Basel and Cologne have to be considered) founders to vend matrices on an international scale. His access to antimony must have been easy and cheap. In 1578 Granjon went to Rome at the call of Pope Gregory XIII to cut exotics for the Press of Cardinal Ferdinand Medici; and that is the last definite statement about him in the reference books, though Baudrier says he ultimately returned to his native Paris. By this time his romans, as well as his italics, had spread throughout Europe.*

Some slight knowledge of italic encouraged the Corporation's adviser in 1922 to regard the fount used at the Imprimerie Nationale in association with the 'Garamond' roman as uncontemporary in appearance. It was not discoverable in the early productions of the Imprimerie Royale, though it makes its appearance within a few years of its foundation. Moreover, as engraving, the related italic does not equal the quality of roman. Accordingly, the Corporation was advised to rely upon the earlier, and not the later, italics used at the Louvre. The italic used in series 156 is based on that used in

the Imprimerie Royale in 1640. As the original used for the pur-
pose was composed in the size of 'gros canon' (about 36-point) the
Corporation arranged its first size of roman and italic for key-
boarding, and casting on a large body, in fact 24-point.* From the
manufacturing point of view the italic is a remarkable achievement,
for so scriptorial a design had not so far been cut for mechanical
composition. The ligatures included all the long ſ sorts and their
combinations, as well as some forty terminal sorts, including, besides
those shown in this composition, the following: Ex, Qu, Qu, gg, gy,
ij, qȝ, and a fine & (ampersand).

The reproduced fount is a satisfactory facsimile of a difficult
original, of which it may be said with accuracy that it belongs to
the second generation of fine French typography, i.e. 1510–60. It is
a period about which more is known of the biography, less of the
bibliography, of the printers and publishers. Ellic Howe's useful
contribution 'The Le Bé Family, 1525–1730' in no. 8 of 'Signature'
(London, March 1938), remarked that the inventory of his father's
stock, which the second Le Bé made about 1598, 'rassemblé par
lui-même et annoté de sa main' (according to Fournier le jeune),
had 'unfortunately disappeared'. It is now known that a copy sur-
vives of the inventory made in 1730 when the daughters of Le Bé sold
the foundry to Fournier l'aîné. The document, which has been drawn
upon in the preceding paragraphs, lists the material (moulds,
punches, matrices); categories (roman, italic, civilité, greek, music,
vignettes, fleurons); sizes (gros canon to nonpareille); and the names
of their engravers (Augereau, Garamond, Granjon, Haultin,
Danfrie and others).

Investigation, hitherto impossible, may now be made into
the origins of the typographical material used in Paris by,
and since, Colines. It is unfortunate that the inventory provides no dates of the cutting of the material listed. However, we must be grateful that the existence of the document
is now known. It is signed by Angelique Le Bé, Marie M.
Le Bé and Anne Catherine Dion *veuve* Fournier (the widow

of Jean Claude Fournier, and mother of Jean Pierre Fournier, who also signs). It comprises 119 sets of matrices, 50 sets of punches, 20 matrices of scripts, and other odds and ends. All, including the Garamond and Granjon punches and matrices, became the property of the elder Fournier: Jean Pierre.

The Monotype movement which began in 1922 and revived the fame and founts of the great masters of the roman letters of fifteenth-century Venice and sixteenth-century Paris, in due time rendered tardy justice to the greatest of all the eighteenth-century French masters, J. P. Fournier's younger brother: Pierre Simon, whose design, as reconstructed, is described in the next following pages.

PIERRE SIMON
FOURNIER LE JEUNE

FIRST RECUT IN 1925 BY THE
MONOTYPE CORPORATION

IERRE SIMON FOURNIER is not appreciated as he deserves in his native country, because the French bibliophile is less interested in what is old than in what is new; his interest in a prospective addition to his library is governed principally by the novelty of its pictorial illustrations. Unillustrated books make little appeal in Paris.

The first modern recognition of Fournier as an artist was, it is satisfactory to record, offered in Paris—by a typefounder. To a series of body and display founts in the style of the eighteenth century, based on the lettering engraved on the copper plates of Charles-Nicolas Cochin, the famous foundry of Peignot et Compagnie added some of Fournier's decorative capitals and ornaments, and correctly ascribed them. But they were incidental to the recognition of Cochin. The specimen of 'Les Cochins' included only the decorative letters mentioned above, but it mounted them in superb style. Substantial modern appreciation of Fournier's artistic contribution originated with Updike's account of the family in the first volume of his treatise on *Printing Types*, 1922. Six years earlier Fournier's technical achievement had been eulogized by an anglicized Frenchman, part author of that capital work *Typographical Printing Surfaces*. The book was dedicated by Lucien Alphonse Legros and John Cameron Grant to Joseph Moxon and Pierre Simon Fournier, described as the only two men who had hitherto attempted 'with the best contemporary knowledge available, to grapple with the problems of the subject'. Reed's tribute to the value of Fournier's work as an up-to-date manual two centuries after its publication has already been noted.

The history of the family which inherited the old Le Bé material (referred to above on p. 73) may be summarized as follows: Jean Claude Fournier, the father of two boys born respectively in 1707 and 1712, was apprenticed to Jean Cot, the Paris typefounder. In 1698 the elder Fournier went to work in the foundry of the widow of the third Guillaume Le Bé, and became its manager in 1707. As has been seen on a previous page, at his father's death Jean Pierre bought the foundry from the daughters of G. Le Bé III. In 1730, at the age of twenty-three, Jean Pierre thus became the proprietor of the oldest typographical material in France. His younger brother Simon Pierre (or Pierre Simon—the names occur in varying order and both belong to Fournier le jeune) was seventeen. The elder Fournier's position as the inheritor, by purchase, of the ancient materials lends him immediate interest. It was the forceful, ambitious, adventurous and quarrelsome, but withal attractive and effective, younger brother, called Fournier le jeune, who made the personal contributions to the art that has made his name known in modern times. He will, it may be presumed, become justly famous as new documents are published. More information has become accessible since Legros wrote in 1916, Updike in 1922, Paul Beaujon in *The Monotype Recorder*, 1926, and H. G. Carter in *Fournier on Typefounding*, 1930. It will be possible some day to digest the information these writings and the new documents give

76

about the Fournier family; the career and final loss of the historic punches and matrices that the elder Fournier had inherited from Le Bé I; and the new faces and bodies that the younger Fournier created.*

No man of his time accomplished so much as Fournier le jeune. He was disappointed at not being allowed to own a printing press, but he created a mass of designs that is unique in the art. Besides romans and italics, it comprises scripts, music type, vignettes and decoration. These he exhibited in specimens which, for magnificence and taste, surpassed all precedent. The extent of his superiority may be seen if two specimen books of the year 1742 are compared: Fournier's *Modéles des Caractères* and Lamesle's *Épreuves Générales*. He also engaged in controversy, anonymously and publicly, with his brother and with others. As his *Manuel Typographique* proves, he was anxious to be taken for an *érudit*. Its author was certainly an egoist: better artist than scholar.

It is not to be doubted that the younger Fournier was himself the engraver of many of his founts. From 1742 his romans and italics are announced as 'nouvellement gravés by Simon-Pierre Fournier le jeune' and this is acceptable. Although his later work, cut on the very narrow 'poétique' scale developed in Amsterdam, is more economical, it is his early period as a designer, i.e. from 1736, that is the best representation of his powers as an artist. He died in 1768, busy finishing his *Manuel*, when he was fifty-six. Simultaneously Bodoni, then aged twenty-eight, was appointed director of the Stamperia Reale at Parma, where he introduced types and ornaments new to Italy. They came from Fournier, who ranks with Bodoni as a principal formative influence of the century; and before all as a typographic pioneer. He had worked his apprenticeship in Jean Pierre's foundry. The birth of his elder brother's first son, Jean François, made all the difference to him. His instant realization that he could never hope to inherit the old foundry determined him to strike out a new line for himself, and it is the pursuit of this ambition that makes him so interesting a personality in the trade. He was twenty-five years of age when he abandoned the style of the old masters (from whom, nevertheless, he was eager to learn) in order to follow the modern trends.

The scientific commission set up in 1692 to revise the typography of the Imprimerie Royale, the new Dutch fashion, and certain German tendencies of which the Hollanders had taken notice, together inspired a new approach to letter designing. The commission's recommendations were a rationalization of the shape and terminology of letters (roman and italic were abandoned in favour of *droit* and *penché*), of the proportions (the letters were less square and more oblong), of the terminations to the strokes (the head serifs were horizontal and not inclined from right to left), and of perpendicular shading (the circular characters were O instead of **O**). The rationalistic principle is most obvious in the italic, whose inclination is smoothly regular, in place of Garamond's and Granjon's conflicting angularity. Independently, the Dutch and German founders were making narrower and more economical letters.

Fournier's contribution was individual, though not in fact novel. The new scientific style at the Louvre, logically built up from mathematically regular patterns, was in being before Pierre Simon was born. Almost as soon as he became active, he appreciated the implications in the types of the Dutch founders for whom J. M. Fleischman was working. Changes were impending, but not so powerful that Pierre Simon was compelled to follow them. It was when his elder brother had a son, to inherit the punches from the past (see p. 73), that the younger Fournier resolved to adopt the 'logical' and mathematical system. The Louvre gave him a respect for precision. It would be too much to say, with François Gando le jeune, that Pierre Simon copied 'tant bien que mal les caractères du Louvre', but his indebtedness to the Louvre italics is obvious; and it is true, as the younger Gando says, that Pierre Simon did not speak generously of his predecessors. It was not candid to claim that he invented the italic by which he set such store, nor fair to attack others for imitation. Fournier knew as well as anybody that innovation for innovation's sake is no sound principle for a designer of types for use in books. What he did achieve in a short time was to provide for the trade a series of graceful letters, in rational and economic proportions, cut in mathematically graded sizes; and moreover superlatively well presented.

And if he rightly criticized as 'pedantic' the application of mathematics to type-faces, as was done in the 'Louvre' patterns, he was eager to apply scientific method in the right place, i.e. to type bodies upon which the faces are cast.

To these biographical notes a few paragraphs may be added about the book-faces originated by Fournier, which were recut by the Monotype Corporation and immediately acquired for use at Cambridge. Although it was decided in 1922 to proceed with the recutting of one of the roman and italics characteristic of Fournier's early period, work was not begun until the autumn of 1924. When the Corporation made its decision, there remained some doubt as to the best model, and two designs were cut, which are here compared for the first time. They are numbered 185 and 178 respectively.

Owing to some confusion (due to the typographical adviser's absence abroad), series 185 was approved. This, therefore, is the face that, after a highly successful career of over twenty-five years, appears here and in the Corporation's specimen. It is a reproduction of Nos. XLVI (roman) and XLVII (italic) named in the *Manuel Typographique* as 'St Augustin Ordinaire'. The great seven-volume Shakespeare printed at Cambridge for Francis Meynell between 1929 and 1933 is, according to the considered judgement of its designer, the '*chef d'œuvre* of the Nonesuch Press'. As a use of series 185, it is no less a monument to Fournier le jeune, although the capitals were specially reduced in height. The first size of the Monotype recutting was completed in 1925.

The second and, surely, preferable design (shown in this paragraph) is numbered series 178, only one size of which, in one set of matrices, was struck. They were acquired by Cambridge, where they are known as 'Barbou', and were first used for the composition of *The Fleuron*, vol. V, printed at Cambridge in 1926. The Barbou type was used for the composition in 1926 on a type-facsimile of *Traité historique et critique sur l'origine et les progrès des caractères de font, pour l'impression de la musique* which Fournier wrote and Barbou published in 1765. The facsimile was duly proofed, but pressure of work of a different kind having first delayed the writing of the necessary introduction and finally postponed it to the Greek Kalends, Lewis after fifteen years dissed the type ('It had whiskers on it'), and the project was abandoned. The Barbou type has had occasional use since *The Fleuron* came to its appointed end with volume VII (Cambridge, 1930). This paragraph enables comparison to be made with the standard Fournier shown in those preceding it. Both designs were cut by Fournier le jeune before 1742. They are both unmistakably eighteenth-century in cut; neither is conspicuously French, or even markedly continental. Both series provide for a persistent need in the trade: a bookish type which is narrow in the body without looking starved, an effect better reached by series 178 than by 185.*

The headpiece at the beginning of this section is composed from reproductions of ornaments designed and engraved by the artist. Fournier's ornaments as a whole and the use he made of them alone place him at the head of his craft during a century that included Bodoni and Baskerville among his great contemporaries.

THE ROMAN AND *ITALIC* OF
JOHN BASKERVILLE
ORIGINALLY USED FOR THE
WORKS OF VIRGIL, BIRMINGHAM 1757
FIRST RECUT BY THE
MONOTYPE CORPORATION IN 1923

The type now before the reader reproduces the first appearance in print of the style of native letter common among contemporary English writing masters such as George Shelley, the famous master of writing at the Blue Coat School. John Baskerville of Birmingham had himself been one of these professional writing masters. Having later made a fortune in the novel trade of japanning, he reverted to his earlier interest in letters, and in 1750 began to design a type. His first printed book, a quarto Virgil published in 1757, had a great ovation abroad but a somewhat divided reception at home. Nevertheless, the *succès d'estime* which his types enjoyed over the next six years (culminating in the folio Bible printed at Cambridge in 1763) encouraged other founders to imitate them. In 1764 Isaac Moore produced for Fry's typefoundry a series which closely followed Baskerville's model. Flattery without plagiary came from the leading continental type designers, Fournier, Didot and Bodoni. In 1779 Baskerville's types and equipment were sold by his widow to Beaumarchais, but English printers could still, if they wished, buy type of truly native design from his imitators at home. The opportunity was ignored by the majority, who preferred the types of Caslon. Dr Edmund Fry noticed to his regret that his 'improved' versions of Baskerville's type 'did not meet with the encouraging approbation of the Printers' and by 1780 was offering types which followed the shape of Caslon's with such accuracy that they could 'not be distinguished from those of that celebrated founder'. Until the end of the eighteenth century printers and public alike remained satisfied with types cut by Caslon or his imitators.

The first decade of the nineteenth century saw a revolutionary change in typographical taste. Among the *literati* and elsewhere a liking had grown for 'modern' types after the manner of Didot and Bodoni. The few English books produced at the Parma press may have turned the scales. In 1799 *The Times* changed from 'old face' to 'modern', the 'new and beautiful Type being the product of Mrs Caslon's Foundery'. Nine years later* not one of the once admired founts of the originator of the foundry was to be found in the Caslon specimen book. To his disgust Dr Fry saw both his series of 'Baskerville' and 'Caslon' carried to the melting pot.

And when the pendulum began to swing it was Caslon's 'old' face and not Baskerville's that was the first to return to favour. The reason is simple. The Caslon types had enjoyed continuous popularity in Britain from 1734 till past the turn of the century. They had found their way into many printing houses, and though founders may have melted down great quantities of the type, printers did not liquidate their entire stocks. As punches of both the original design and of the numerous imitations were still preserved, there was no difficulty in producing a supply equal to any revival in demand. Caslon's types were displayed again on the title-pages of several books published by Pickering in 1840. Whether the inspiration came from his printer,

Whittingham, or from the joint intelligence of the Pickering-Whittingham alliance is not clear. But it may be asserted that the appearance of Herbert's *Temple* in 1844 and *Lady Willoughby's Diary* published by Longman in the same year marks the beginning of Caslon's return to favour.

Baskerville's memory was kept green by numerous admirers and collectors, but only in France (and there until late in the nineteenth century) did printers continue to boast of using for fine work types cut 'after the manner of Baskerville'. In Britain however the typographical experts could not agree on the merits of his type. Talbot Baines Reed, in a lecture before the Society of Arts in 1890, declared that Baskerville's type was 'one of the most beautiful we have had', but William Morris and Emery Walker found it 'uninteresting and poor' when writing their essay on printing in 1893. By contrast, they found Caslon's type 'clear and neat, and fairly well designed'. Caslon again became the magic name in the better class of English typography. His design was constantly to be seen in books printed at the Chiswick Press, and by the leading Scottish houses. Shaw used it and boomed it.

But Baskerville, in more senses than one, would not lie down. Birmingham's pride in his achievements became more effective between 1861 and 1876 when a local antiquary, Samuel Timmins, avidly collected information about his life and work. In the *fin de siècle* atmosphere of 1893, the second exhumation of his body attracted the interest of a wider public. At Cleveland, Ohio, where the construction of printing presses has a regional importance, a paper on Baskerville was read to the Rowfant Club in 1899. Two years later, a Baskerville Club was founded by enthusiasts at Cambridge University. A copy of this Club's first publication, *A Handlist of Baskerville's Books*, was given to Ralph Straus in 1905 and was incorporated with additions into his memoir of John Baskerville, printed at Cambridge in 1907 for Messrs Chatto and Windus. American interest in the Birmingham printer was stimulated anew by Josiah Benton's paper to the Boston Society of Printers in 1914, handsomely printed in the same year by D. B. Updike at the Merrymount Press.

Between 1910 and 1917, the types cut in imitation of Baskerville's for Fry's foundry were to be found in the specimen books of English and American typefounders. Messrs Stephenson, Blake and Company, into whose possession the punches had come after their absorption of the firm of Sir Charles Reed and Sons in 1905, took pride in issuing a notice in April 1910 offering the roman design, adapted to the lining system and paired to a so-called Georgian italic. The Fry roman was shown again, without cropped ascenders or descenders, in the supplementary catalogue issued in 1917 by the American Type Founders Company. From this source, Frederic Warde obtained a fount for the Princeton University Press, where he was appointed printing manager late in 1921. In the same year, Bruce Rogers made use of a fount of authentic Baskerville type at the Harvard University Press. During his time in Cambridge as typographical adviser, he had identified some type from the Fonderie Bertrand as bearing the true Baskerville design and as being mostly cast from original matrices, but being unable to transact business with France during the war he had to wait until his move to Cambridge, Massachusetts, before ordering a fount of the type from Paris. It remained for the Monotype recutting of Baskerville in 1923 to bring the design for the first time into popular use. By now, Bembo and Baskerville have so decreased the use of 'old face' that it is possible that Caslon, after so long an innings, will become obsolete. Baskerville cannot be said to be more picturesque than Caslon, but its proportions are better, the face is clearer and the whole design, roman and italic (upon which see the paragraph at the foot of this page), more efficient for present-day work.

That the need for a round, open type was widely felt is confirmed by the fact that, when the Corporation's facsimile was publicized, foundries and composing-machine companies in America and Germany followed with similar revivals. Yet there is to be noted a great disparity in the appearance of these revivals. When John Baskerville cut his seventeen sizes of type for text, titling and display, he varied the proportions and even the pattern of his letters to an unusual degree from one size to the next. These variations were not followed in the Monotype recutting, which took as a model for all sizes the great primer design used by Baskerville in his finest books, the quarto classics and the folio Bible. The Monotype series judiciously produced on this model was to prove of greater utility to the trade than any of the other types named after Baskerville, introduced between 1925 and 1929. Of these, the Stempel Foundry's recutting was the more faithful in the smaller sizes, whilst the Linotype version, launched in 1929 with a 14-point size, had the advantage of being directly adapted from a fount of type cast mostly from true Baskerville matrices struck for the size he cast on English body.

It is not so easy to be enthusiastic about Baskerville's italic. There is neatness, modesty and consistency in the design but it is lacking in nobility, picturesqueness and character. The capitals of the italic are regular in slope and combine well—no mean advantage over Caslon's. The lower case is a fraction too narrow to permit of elegance. Fry's italics are a decided improvement upon Baskerville's. But it is not to be denied that, all deficiencies apart, the design as a whole possesses a degree of efficiency well worthy of Birmingham.

The Press acquired the Monotype series in 1924 and has employed it as a standard book type ever since. One of the earliest books in which it appeared was, appropriately, an edition of Milton's *Paradise Regained* printed for *The Fleuron* in that same year; and it was used in 1926 for the *Journals of T. J. Cobden-Sanderson*, issued in two volumes. The special pride and interest that Cambridge takes in Baskerville's design was recently rewarded by the great generosity of Monsieur Charles Peignot in presenting to the Press the original punches, acquired by his firm in 1936.

The prophecy may confidently be made that the neglect into which Baskerville's name was allowed to fall is at an end and that his design will retain its already established position as one of the half-dozen standard book and jobbing founts of the world.

THE ROMAN AND *ITALIC* OF

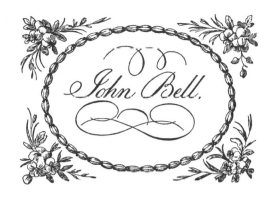

FIRST CUT AT
BELL's BRITISH LETTER
FOUNDRY IN 1788

RECUT BY THE
MONOTYPE CORPORATION IN 1930

THE second English eighteenth-century face recut by Monotype composition at this period was the design originally
engraved by Richard Austin for John Bell. While Baskerville
is rounder than Caslon, Bell is narrower. It is as undeniably
English in appearance as Baskerville, though its proportions
are deliberately French. Bell was often in Paris persuading
with success Moreau le jeune and other leaders of the Paris
school of illustrators to engrave the frontispieces for the
British Theatre and his other publications. And, although
Bell did not engage in typefounding until twenty years after
the death of Pierre Simon Fournier, it is extremely probable
that he was acquainted with his specimens and with those
of others, like François Ambroise Didot, who followed the

87

proportions of Fournier's letters. Bell himself says that he had 'examined and compared the Types of every Foundry in Europe'. There is indeed evidence in 1786 that he had actually brought over a contemporary French italic type of obvious Didot design. But Bell's own design, apart from the proportions of the letters, was deliberately 'British', intended to be cast at the British Letter Foundry for the publication of Bell's British Library, and 'to retrieve and exalt the neglected art of printing in England'.

Bell's collaborator, Austin, served him well. As a professional engraver on copper and wood, he imparted a note of brilliance, rare at the time, to the British punches he cut for Bell. As displayed on the smooth handmade paper of his thin quartos the type looks much more 'elegant' than its predecessors. Bell's use of paper and ink, and his recourse to Paris for the illustrators of his editions, prove that he had learned much from Baskerville. Yet the 'British' type departs in numerous details and in general style from all precedent, continental and insular. No letters hitherto cut had been finished off as in the manner of the British Letter Foundry's roman and italic of 1789. The sharpness of the taper given to all the serifs was new in typefounding. It was the greatest development in 'finish' that had occurred since Aldus substituted his bracketed for Jenson's flat serif. Both Fleischman and F. A. Didot kept their serifs relatively blunt. At this time Bodoni followed their practice.* The finely tapered and bracketed serif of Bell and Austin became in due time an essential part of the modern Anglo-Scottish practice. There is no difference between the 'idea' of the paragon that Austin cut for Bell in 1788 and that of the so-called 'Scotch Roman' the same engraver cut for the Edinburgh founders twenty years later, which is the basis of the 'moderns' most widely used today, e.g. Monotype series 7. This is the 'modern' that Cambridge has long used for the great mass of its scientific work, including the composition of many journals of the learned societies. The British Letter Foundry's roman and italic was a fine piece of engraving.

The innovation for which Bell and Austin were responsible was far greater than was realized at the time or has since been admitted. The creators of the first modern face do not seem to have secured much contemporary use for the type. The sumptuous edition of the *Book of Common Prayer* that Bell intended as its monument was abandoned—at the pressure, no doubt, of the King's Printer. Doubtless, too, Bell's peculiar methods of business partly accounted for the failure to establish the type. There may have been a quarrel, for Bell did not himself make much use of the pica or long primer in his books. But Bell's new daily newspaper *The Oracle* (1789) ranks as the most elegant sheet ever published, surpassing even *The World* (1787) for which he and Topham had been responsible. *The Oracle* makes a brilliant appearance in layout, paper and presswork, and in all the sizes so far cut of the new type, i.e. from paragon to long primer. But the newspaper trade was expanding, competition was keen and bourgeois was being increasingly used in the advertising columns. The British Letter Foundry had no bourgeois. By 1794 Bell lost *The Oracle* and three years afterwards the Foundry was dissolved and the first modern type forgotten, not to be seen again in England until 1930.

Bell's types found greater appreciation in the United States. They were seen in Massachusetts in 1792, Pennsylvania in 1795 and their use can be traced in New York in 1800. Thereafter occurs a break of over fifty years, during which the trade took to the later founts of Austin, Thorne and others. In 1864, however, Henry Oscar Houghton of Boston was in England collecting compositors and materials for the series of fine editions he was planning to produce at the Riverside Press. Among the material Houghton brought back with him was a set of Bell's types cast from the original punches and matrices of Bell's British Letter Foundry. These had descended, by purchase, to Stephenson, Blake and Company, the celebrated founders of Sheffield.

The Riverside Press enterprise prospered and broadened. In 1880, Daniel Berkeley Updike came, like every other beginner at the Riverside Press, as an errand boy. After twelve years in other capacities he had earned a respect for his typographical talent, and was desirous of exercising it independently. A little book *Vexilla Regis* appeared. It was 'Printed for the compiler at the Riverside Press, Cambridge, under the supervision of D. B. Updike, Six Beacon Street, Boston'. Updike had set up the office that was to become famous as the Merrymount Press. This was in the year 1893.

In 1895 Houghton died, leaving his partner, George H. Mifflin, to succeed to the direction of the Riverside Press. At this point Bruce Rogers was attracted to the Press and given responsibility for design. Rogers soon perceived the merits of the types that Houghton had purchased thirty years earlier.* They were used for an edition of Mackail's translation of the *Georgics* printed at the Riverside Press in 1904. The types were then known at the Riverside Press under the name of the well-known Bostonian writer, Martin Brimmer, for whom the firm had acted as publishers. Updike admired these types while he was with the Riverside Press. After tracing their history until he found which British typefoundry owned the matrices, he obtained strikes for his own casting. He named his new founts 'Mountjoye', and made consistent use of them from 1903 onwards, an exacting test for any design.

In 1926 research into other subjects occasioned the chance examination in the Bibliothèque Nationale of the unique (as it was discovered to be) copy of the 'Address to the World by Mr Bell, British-Library, Strand, London'. It was immediately recognized to be composed in the 'Brimmer' or the 'Mountjoye' types. Their true origin thus became known for the first time since 1788. The 'Address' was reproduced in *John Bell 1745–1831* (Cambridge, 1930), composed with new founts cast from the original material by Stephenson, Blake and Company. The book stimulated the interest of book collectors, and in 1931 the First Edition Club arranged an exhibition which included *The British Theatre* and *The British Poets*, Bell's serial publications, remarkable for their engraved illustrations as well as for their typographical style. The newspapers in which he had an interest were also shown, beginning with the *Morning Post* and *The Oracle*, and ending with *Bell's Weekly Messenger*. The exhibition, of course, included *La Belle Assemblée*, the celebrated magazine of fashion 'addressed particularly to the Ladies'. A worthy catalogue of the exhibits was printed at Cambridge. The debt to John Bell was at last recognized. But it remained to set up a memorial more enduring than an exhibition.

A Monotype facsimile of the original was made with the collaboration of Stephenson, Blake and Company. The first size was completed in 1931. It is an admirable reproduction and a practical contribution to the contemporary book trade, as was proved by its first use for the text of *The English Newspaper* (Cambridge, 1932). The design was later cut by the independent American Monotype organization. Monotype Bell has since established itself in the esteem of those in the habit of printing the 'literary' sort of book. The economic proportions that Bell adopted indirectly from Fournier fit it for work whose extent makes a very compact but highly legible type desirable. It combines this utilitarian virtue with a note of elegance lacking in any other 'modern' face. For sheer brilliance of cutting, that is to say fineness of serif, it is comparable only with Eric Gill's Perpetua.

GOUDY MODERN
ROMAN & *ITALIC*

FIRST CUT
FOR HAND COMPOSITION
1918
RECUT BY THE MONOTYPE CORPORATION
1928

The design now in front of the reader combines interesting variations on several calligraphical and typographical themes. The roman is of French eighteenth and the italic of English nineteenth century inspiration; and the roman does not derive from a typographical exemplar while the italic does. The most conspicuous element of both is their weight, which is that of Bodoni's late classical period. A second patent characteristic is the relative height of the capitals to the lower case, which is that of the early Italian renaissance. In the designer's hands, however, this roman and italic have been so thoroughly anglicized and modernized that the face requires classification as an English early nineteenth-century face. While not, strictly speaking, a book-type, it can be used for texts, even of great length, as may be seen in the Nonesuch *Don Quixote* printed at Cambridge in 1930 in the 12-point size, or in the second Nonesuch Shakespeare recently published. But while it is admirably serviceable for limited editions, it finds its best general employment in certain kinds of extra-literary composition as, for example, catalogues and prospectuses.

A collection of some interest might be made of the addresses and diplomas, the placards and posters printed at Cambridge in the early years of Lewis's period. During this time new founts for hand composition were bought from typefounders at home and abroad, among them being 'Cloister' and 'Goudy Old Style' from the American Type Founders Company. It is not so easy today to realize the paucity of new types, book or jobbing, literary or commercial, in the 1920's. The Old Style just referred to was one of the best designs available and has its use today. Cambridge acquired a full range of it and employed it for every kind of advertising and propaganda. The Modern type here seen is Monotype set, but it is available also for hand composition from Stephenson, Blake and Company, as the successors to the historic house of Caslon, with whom Goudy at the effective period had relations. It was cut as part of the Monotype programme of 1922.

The 1922 programme, it may perhaps be usefully repeated at this point, was only in part revivalist. At the time there were good reasons for making facsimiles of designs that have been lost for bad reasons. But, it was hoped, the programme would in the course of time and the increase of experience make available designs by practising artists as well as those of old masters. It led, as will be seen, to the cutting of the Perpetua design of Eric Gill, as well as his Sans. It was also designed to make this programme international in its scope. In after years (not touched in this book) designs by French,

93

Dutch and German designers were cut. In the first instance it was natural to turn to America and to the most versatile and successful type designer of that country, and to secure from his hand a face that would be attractive and give distinction to contemporary advertising and book production. Of the many designs made and cut by Frederic William Goudy (1865–1947) the present is most suited to work requiring a moderate inflection of style. Even in advertising it is desirable for a type design to be conservative, and some deliberately 'conservative' designs made for the composition of books are better suited to advertising. The 'Cheltenham' of Bertram Goodhue is an instance and in Frederic Goudy's list there are many such: the famous Kennerley is one, and the version he made of the 'Garamont' or Caractères de l'Université (see above, pp. 61ff.) is another.

The difficulty of designing a completely new face that will serve the composition of every kind of book over a considerable period, say half a century or more, is well illustrated by the career of Frederic William Goudy, a great name in printing as well as in type design.

Goudy became interested in printing at the same period in which the interest of Updike and Rogers was quickened. But the difference in Goudy's case was that he was as much a lettering artist as he was a printer. From 1896 he began the connections with the typefounders which he maintained for many years, during which he designed Kennerley Old Style and the Forum and Hadriano capitals. He printed very handsome specimens of his founts and wrote and printed expositions of his principles of design. Although he was so active a printer, in the private press sense, he became attached to the American Monotype Company in the capacity of Art Director in 1920. This, however, did not exhaust his interest in design. He continued to design and cut faces of his own, for hand composition. The present is one of these.

94

It was first used in the summer of 1918, when the second number of *Ars Typographica*, edited by Goudy, was composed by hand in the 18-point size cast at his Village Letter Foundery. In 1928 a 12-point was cut for machine composition by the Monotype Corporation, and made its first appearance at Cambridge in an effectively set up Autumn Announcement List for 1929, where the design appears to fine advantage.

The design of the roman capitals and lower case is a robust rendering of some of the letters used by the French engravers of the eighteenth century for the names, dedications, etc., added to the plates of their portraits, pictures and even odd jobs. The forms which inspired Goudy may be seen on the title-page of La Borde's *Choix de Chansons* (Paris, 1773) which shows several lines of these capitals and of the roman lower case. Goudy's type is a very free rendering of the French design, and takes no pains to preserve the artificiality of the engraver's sharpness of contrast between the thicks and thins. That the face is French in inspiration is made obvious by the retention of the lower case 'b' with the foot serif at the left, a trick that Grandjean had started and Fournier le jeune had popularized. It is now almost a French fetish. The Goudy roman has exceptionally long projectors. These have the remarkable effect of shrinking the height of the normal lower case so that the 12-point, say, appears the equivalent of 10-point in The Times New Roman. The capitals are short, as in Italian fifteenth-century calligraphy.

The italic is not French but English in inspiration, as may better be seen if it is compared with the work of William Bulmer. The face cannot be regarded today as above criticism. The projectors are excessively long for the smaller sizes and the capitals excessively short. It was a mistake to reproduce in the Monotype version these eccentricities, pardonable or even agreeable as they are in private press printing, where

95

experimental typography is not only justifiable but desirable. In the 1920's there had been much discussion of the ideal proportions of roman lettering: the writing of Antonio Sinibaldi, the celebrated scribe who worked for the rich collectors of Florence and Naples in the last quarter of the fifteenth century, had been pointed to as representing the *ne plus ultra* of humanistic script.* The type has the short capitals and long projectors of this handsome script, and it can be claimed that, in a comparable size, the type possesses much of the elegance of the fifteenth-century Italian script, the brilliance of eighteenth-century French engraving and the regularity of nineteenth-century English cutting. The reproduction was made from the original types supplied by Goudy.

PERPETUA   ROMAN &

FELICITY ITALIC

CUT FOR MONOTYPE COMPOSITION

1929

THE commercial value of the new Monotype programme had been abundantly proved within five years by the sales of Garamond, Polifilo, and Baskerville. It has been seen that the programme had been accepted in 1922 by H. M. Duncan without any regard to prospect of profit, but as a duty and a service owed by a monopoly concern to the trade which had carried it to prosperity. Duncan's successors were less enthusiastically idealist and for the reasons given above (see p. 33) it was fortunate that the sales of the faces cut between 1922 and 1928 were satisfactory, and more.

Consistently with the intentions formed in 1922 it still remained desirable to cut for the book-trade an original face —one that should not be another old master such as Bembo, nor a redrawn classic such as Centaur—but a wholly new design corresponding with contemporary demands. Such a desire to round off the programme by the cutting of a new roman and italic for book-work required a living artist capable of the work. There was no lack of fine calligraphers or fine printers in Britain and Germany. It has been remarked earlier that out of the vast number of the romans cut in Germany in response to the inspiration of the Kelmscott and Doves Presses only one has established itself: Weiss Antiqua. The rest were all too personal and exhibited too much self-consciousness to be good in any respect, save for the most limited use in a private press. In Britain the great Johnstonian calligraphical movement, which had been followed so closely and keenly in Germany, had produced writing comparable with the best of the best periods. The broad pen was employed to provide large fine uncials, half-uncials and minuscules. The writing of long texts in small sizes of letter was rare. The inspiration was medieval and many of the scribes (not Johnston himself, particularly) were anti-renaissance in outlook. The possibility was remote of securing from this source a satisfactory set of drawings of a new roman and italic suitable for work of every sort.

Thus there seemed to be no reason to suppose that the English calligraphic artist would succeed where the German professor failed. The typographic artists, independent of Johnston, had also not produced any founts of which the trade could make use. The work of T. J. Cobden-Sanderson, Herbert Horne, Charles Ricketts and other leaders of the later English private press movement was also too individualistic to be of permanent value. With the possible exception of the Doves and Golden types, their efforts had been new and peculiar as well as private. What was wanted was a design that, while being new, was of general utility and in no respect unusual. To secure a set of such drawings was the first great difficulty that required to be faced if this part of the Corporation's plan were to be achieved. The essence of the difficulty lies in the fact that types for modern books still require to be serifed throughout both the roman and italic. In vain have the intellectuals, principally German and Swiss, endeavoured to establish sans-serif as the type of 'our' time. The superior legibility of serifed against un-serifed types is too obvious to justify delaying the reader with any criticism of 'die neue Typographie'. This does not mean that sans-serif has no use, but that its right use is a problem. That a sans-serif type by a contemporary practitioner of lettering could be rightly employed had been proved when types from Edward Johnston's drawings were cut for Frank Pick and the Underground Railway in 1916; and again when Eric Gill made a sans-serif which the Monotype Corporation cut in 1928 and used for certain kinds of advertising. This 'sans' was a sensational success and has established itself in the trade as essential to the composition of certain kinds of commercial book, i.e. time-tables, guide-books, catalogues, etc. In this sense it is a twentieth-century type. It owes its success as a design to the pioneer 'sans' of Johnston, behind whom stood Gerard Meynell. It was he who persuaded Frank Pick to commission the Johnston 'sans', and to standardize it for use in the publicity of the Underground Railway. This was a highly significant accomplishment in 1916 but there was no essential difficulty about it.

The situation is very different when a calligrapher of the Johnstonian school sets out to design a type for use in books intended to be read by the broad literary public. Furthermore there remained the problem of what to do with such a design when it had been secured. No such problem occurred with Gill's sans-serif, the first size of which had been cut by June 1928, and this was an original design. The competence of the Corporation to make, either from prints or types, facsimiles of 'classic' faces of the past had been proved; so now was its competence to use a modern artist's drawings of a sans-serif. Long before, the Corporation had cut punches from new drawings made for the purpose by draughtsmen capable of making clear outlines. But as to a book-type of the highest ambition, no reproduction direct from the drawing-board had been as satisfactory as those made from type already existing, e.g. Bell's roman and italic. The difference between the drawn pattern and the engraved letter was crucial. Virtue went out with the hand-cutter when the mechanic came in with his pantograph and the rest of the gear. The new engineers were not what the old engravers were. They could mass-produce, or reproduce, punches; they could not create, or recreate, the engraved quality that had belonged to typography in the roman letter since 1465.

The crispness of line and smoothness of curve, combined with a just contrast between the thick and thin strokes, was a virtue implicit in the faces that came from the hand of Griffo, Lautizio, Garamond, Granjon, Fournier and Austin. Some of this virtue lay implicit in the script upon which they modelled their shapes. It was, indeed, the task of these engravers to make these virtues explicit. Roman serifed type is less a new dimension of script than a translation of writing into engraving. And the substitution of an engraved for a written letter is part of the tradition of four centuries; it is irreversible, and will hold equally if and when a photographed image is substituted for cast type.

But the quality that only engraving can confer is more than a concomitant of this long tradition in typography. It is an essential factor in a quality to which that tradition is a witness, and possesses prior importance: legibility. The finely bracketed serif with which the sculptors of the roman inscriptions digni-fied their alphabet is symbolic; it signified their sense of the fundamental difference between private and public writing; between script and inscription. Thus the function of the serif must be understood by the artist if his book-type is to have a chance of succeeding. The fine serif is not in origin calligraphic but epigraphic; not written but sculptured. It follows that a set of drawings of a finely serifed type by a contemporary practitioner of lettering could best be made by one who was either an engraver on metal or wood; or, preferably, a sculptor on stone or slate. On this analysis the problem became soluble, and Gill was the obvious man to solve it. He was asked to make drawings of the letters he had long been habitually carving. When they were ready they were not given forthwith to the

Monotype works as those for Gill Sans had been. It was intended to preserve absolutely the chiselled quality of Gill's capitals and lower case, and for this reason it was decided not to make a direct photographic and pantographic reproduction of the drawings. Instead, they were given to Charles Malin of Paris. A set of punches in upper and lower case in 12-point Didot was cut in May 1926 and a set of titling capitals in October of the same year. Matrices were struck and type cast by Ribadeau Dumas, the Paris typefounder. Some important corrections were made; notably f, y, were recut. Later, all the punches were brought to London and used to serve the process of reproduction for composing-machine purposes, just as the original Bell types of Stephenson, Blake and Company had been.*

As the original Malin punches of the upper and lower case fount, now known as Monotype series 239, were cut on a cicero body according to the Didot scale, which on the Anglo-American system is equivalent to 13-point, the first size completed by the Monotype was also 13-point, a peculiar size, most unwelcome to the English trade. But the project was proceeded with. Malin also cut some sizes of capitals for use as titling founts, and these undoubtedly are the most successful of all. Later a light and a bold were cut, building up to the range of series now established as one of the fine faces of the world. The first size of the upper and lower case roman in Monotype was completed in August 1928. The first specimen was a private print of the English translation, made for the purpose by Walter Shewring, of *The Passion of Perpetua and Felicity* who were martyred at Carthage in the year 203. The roman was named 'Perpetua', and the italic cut later 'Felicity'.

The first public use of the roman was made at Cambridge, for the composition of Eric Gill's *Art-Nonsense* published by Messrs Cassell in December 1929. As the italic had not then been completed, the author's emphasis is expressed by underlining, a desperate (and unique) device which is at least preferable to the German habit of spacing lower-case letters.

When the italic appeared it was slightly less monumental than might have been expected; capitals, D, J and R, were cursive, while the lower case was less cursive—though a, f, g, were orthodox, and p, m, n, were serifed. The rest of the sorts were strongly romanized. Much trouble was taken over f. Finally f was adopted. The Felicity italic is the outcome of a number of compromises. Most of the capitals and many of the lower case are inclined monumental characters, the few capitals indicated above are cursive. The theoretical discussion about 'sloped roman' had not been without its influence on the italic but the rejection of f in favour of f proves that the calligraphic past of italic was still robust and capable of holding its position in the typography of the future.

The full alphabet of the lower case, i.e. the roman and the italic, with the titling capitals, form a consistent whole. The equality of serif treatment throughout makes for a notable degree of harmony between all the characters, which is supported by the element of formal cursive which underlies the roman lower case and the element of current cursive which underlies the italic lower case. Both lower case and capitals are at their best in the display sizes.

Not surprisingly, the complete 13-point size appears at its best in a book written and illustrated by the designer. In *Clothes* (London, Jonathan Cape, 1931), printed at Cambridge, on a page measuring $7\frac{1}{2} \times 4\frac{1}{8}$ inches, the main strokes of the Perpetua text are sturdy enough to bear the artist's constant resort to a white line on solid ground, and hence the cuts harmonize with the type hardly less well than the Polifilo cuts with Aldus's third roman. This harmony is not apparent to the same degree in *The Passion of Perpetua and Felicity*, a quarto set to a measure which necessitates leading. The fount used in the *Passion* is of extra interest, as it uses, at the beginning and middle of words, the alternative lower-case 'y' with a straight terminal, and as a terminal, the tailed 'y'—probably the only occasion on which the experiment was made. In the hand-cut version only the straight-tailed 'y' was cut; in the final Monotype version as produced for the trade, the curved-tailed 'y' is supplied.

It may safely be prophesied that the titling capitals, i.e. series 258 (which reproduces the punches cut by Malin), will be esteemed as long as the Latin alphabet remains the basis of western recorded civilization. The lower case of the display sizes from 30-point to 72-point is also magnificent, especially

PERPETUA
showing thirty point

the roman. And this is natural, inevitable. The design originated in Gill's inscriptional lettering, not in a book-script, for he had none. Had it been possible for him to be interested enough in calligraphy to transcribe books in the equivalent of 16-point or, better, 12-point, it is abundantly possible that his Perpetua would have realized to the maximum the intentions of its producers.

Obviously from the composition at present before the reader the bodies 14-point and below, i.e. the 'book sizes', are suitable for the composition of long texts in a wide variety of categories. The lower case is undeniably distinguished in appearance and comfortably readable in mass. But the question whether the sizes 8-point to 14-point fully realize the ambition with which they were begun, i.e. to create an original type serviceable for all kinds of books, does not permit of an answer in the unqualified affirmative. Perpetua, it may be said at once, is eminently suitable for certain kinds of books; those less commonly produced now than when the design was cut—nearly twenty-five years ago. But apart from the fact that the proportions of the letters correspond with the economic situation of 1929, which no longer generally obtains, the design expresses a note of particularity and self-consciousness not universally acceptable. For work of a scientific character, it is possible that the type looks not merely distinguished but too distinguished. In such printing the effect is more artistic or literary than is wanted.

Hence Perpetua is a design appropriate for select classes of work with which a certain obvious degree of 'style' is desired, as for example, the semi-private printing with which Gill was for a long time intimately associated. While the relations of the thicks and thins and the serifs are perfectly judged, and all the essentials are present in correct balance, certain departures from the norm, set up by centuries, distract and therefore estrange the reader, though only to a slight extent. The characters a, d, f, r, depart minutely from the absolute convention established since Aldus. And this is a welcome innovation in the large sizes, but the same variations repeated, few though they are, in the small sizes, suffice to render the design 'peculiar'. None of this is, after all, surprising. A sculptor does not work in small sizes, and is not compelled to regard the economic use of space as his first law. It must follow that any letters he cuts and a typefounder reproduces will look their best not in small sizes in books but in large sizes in placards. Perpetua may be judged in the small sizes to have achieved the object of providing a distinguished form for a distinguished text; and, in the large sizes, a noble, monumental, appearance.

THE NEW ROMAN
AND ITALIC

DESIGNED IN
PRINTING HOUSE SQUARE FOR

THE ❦ TIMES

IN 1931

The volume of comment bestowed elsewhere upon this face dispenses the entry here from everything but a summary description. The design itself may reasonably be taken as familiar even to the non-technical reader. The following paragraphs are set in the type as it was originally cut and in the size employed for *The Times* leading articles. The idea of designing a face to correspond with

the specific needs of the newspaper was first thrown up in 1929 by work done in connection with the Printing Number of *The Times*, published on 29 October 1929. In 1930 experiments were made with the existing faces thought most suitable, Baskerville, Plantin, Imprint, Ionic and others. A special size of Perpetua was cut and a page of *The Times* composed in it. Finally, it was decided to put in hand a new design to be excogitated by Morison, who had entered into relationship with Printing House Square early in 1929. He pencilled the original set of drawings, and handed them to Victor Lardent, a draughtsman in the publicity department of Printing House Square whom he considered capable of producing an unusually firm and lean line. Lardent made a first-class set of finished drawings of the capitals and lower case out of the pencilled patterns given him. These drawings were furnished to the Corporation who cut the punches.* From these the Linotype and Intertype Companies later made their copies. The total number of punches cut by the Monotype for the founts, slug or single-type used in *The Times* of 3 October 1932 was above 14,750, including those recut on account of errors in engraving or second thoughts on the part of the designer. To this number should be added the number of punches cut by the Linotype. Also there were the titlings. These comprised three varieties of capitals (heavy condensed, light wide, heavy wide), five sizes (5½-, 7-, 9-, 11- and 12-point) of text type in roman and italic and small capitals, a roman capital and lower-case bold face in four sizes (7-, 9-, 11- and 12-point) and a large number of special characters for advertisements, Stock Exchange quotations, etc. The designs of all the new titlings were obtained by the thickening, condensing and otherise modifying the main-strokes of the capitals of the text type. The series, since greatly added to in the interests of the trade as a whole, at home and abroad, is a graded, harmonious corpus of types having a range that is unique in typefounding history.

The revision, therefore, was thorough. The only face that survived from the preceding style of the newspaper was the Perpetua titling, regularly used for the picture page. The revision was as satisfactory as it was thorough. There has been no reversion since to the early Victorian design. Hence the Times New Roman has been used throughout the newspaper with no change from the date of its original use, a period of twenty-one years. The face has also served the *Literary Supplement* and all the numerous subsidiary publications issued from Printing House Square throughout the period. In the interval it has established itself as essential to the composition of all manner of newspapers, magazines, advertisements and books of every kind including academic productions.

It is obvious from the matter set in single column above that the design is narrow and therefore economical. The Times New Roman was freed from control in 1933 but took its place at Cambridge in the previous year when it was used for the composition of a special number of the *Monotype Recorder* devoted to the design. It has justified itself as the most acceptable of all contemporary faces for the composition of large standard texts, e.g. of the *Statutes and Ordinances of the University of Cambridge*, which contains over 400,000 words. The criteria of choice which resulted in the final selection of this face for the *Statutes and Ordinances* were to some extent new. Since 1939 it has been necessary for books to be accommodated to the cramped spatial dimensions that had been common to newspapers since the seventeenth century. Hence, the face under consideration, designed as it had been for a newspaper, was found peculiarly appropriate for the extensive post-war manuscript, whose pages and price needed to be kept down. As the economic utility of The Times type exceeded (and exceeds) that of any substitute, it could hardly be resisted by the majority to whom consistently rising costs were a serious consideration. It is safe to say that The Times New Roman will bear the main burden of composition until prices drop. The face is already the most successful, in Britain and in Europe, of all those cut in recent years by any typefounding or composing machine company. Despite its humble origin as a mere newspaper face, it won its way into Mr Updike's office. Top American appreciation has been given to it by its use from 1942 for the text of *Collier's Magazine*, the *Woman's Home Companion* and the *American Magazine*. In June 1953 it was adopted for the *Sun-Times*, the Chicago daily newspaper. If any face can be described as of the twentieth century it is that under consideration. The design has also been adopted for use in conditions which differ from those of newspaper printing. A wide version, more suited to longer lines, is here before the reader's eye. A semi-bold version of the face was originally cut in 7-point for a Bible printed at Cambridge in 1936, and this has proved particularly useful in dictionaries, time-tables and the like.

Morris would have denounced the heresy of the original cutting immediately. As a new face it should, by the grace of God and the art of man, have been broad and open, generous and ample; instead, by the vice of Mammon and the misery of the machine, it is bigoted and narrow, mean and puritan. Notoriously, in his own day, Morris's judgement of letters and lettering was that of an intolerant medievalist, and an admirer of the colour and decoration of the manuscripts written in the thirteenth and four-teenth centuries and the woodcut books of the fifteenth. He did not know as much about printed books as he knew about manuscripts, or as much about lettering as he knew about decoration. Not that his knowledge of either was second-hand; he was no preacher who could, or would, not practise. Yet as a decorator he never seized the significance of printing as a means by which decoration could be disseminated among the widest public. Morris, who understood much, never understood that the great Bibles written in the eighth century were the efforts of missionaries. It did not occur to him that the monks of Corbie, St Gall and Tours would as willingly have set their hands to the punch as to the pen if they could there-by have given the Bible and the Missal to all who could profit by them. Morris's dependence upon Ruskin and his antagonism to the capitalist system prevented his re-cognizing the fact that the 'machine' was bringing the Bible, Liturgy and Literature into the hands of more and more people. It was with the aid of the punch, the matrix and the type, the paper and the press, that for the first time in the history of the world the book became possible as a private possession, entailing universal literacy and much else. The real 'art' was multiplication.

But irrespective of multiplication, any medium of which letters or lettering is part has an innate tendency to be-come a work of art, as Morris rightly said. Since by its essence and nature, typography is a means of multiplica-tion, the art of the letter form it uses must serve that means to that end. Now it is also, and obviously, of the essence of multiplication that it should have an object outside itself. That is to say, the end of typography is multiplication for the sake of man. Just as the text as written must be related to man's intellectual resources, so must the text as printed be related to his pecuniary resources. Yet the essential service that typography renders to man was that derided by Morris as a mere truckling to commercialism. The contrary is the fact. The invention of round faces of wide set, composed in large sizes and printed on handmade paper in a limited edition of copies, may equally be a form of commercialism.

It must be the object of typography, whether practised under nineteenth-century capitalism or twentieth-century pseudo-communism, to multiply the greatest number of copies at the least cost, and The Times type complies with this requirement.*

APPENDIX

BY

NETTY HOEFLAKE, HARRY CARTER
& JOHN DREYFUS

The articles on pages 41–109 were written by Stanley Morison and specifically refer to the book-types introduced at Cambridge between 1922 and 1932. During the inter-war years the Monotype Corporation produced three other types which were subsequently used at Cambridge. Two were classical revivals, Van Dijck and Ehrhardt; the third an original design, Romulus, by the Dutch typographer Jan van Krimpen. Of these three, only Ehrhardt has been installed at Cambridge in a full range of sizes.

VAN DIJCK

First cut c. 1660; recut by the Monotype Corporation in 1937-38

Monotype 'Van Dijck' is named after the famous seventeenth-century Dutch punchcutter Christoffel van Dyck, to whom the original roman and italic can be ascribed. It is an adaptation of the *Augustijn Romeyn* (English-bodied roman) shewn in the specimen which the widow of Daniel Elsevier issued as a sale-catalogue in 1681. Jan van Krimpen identified this face with the roman used in Vondel's Dutch version of Ovid's *Metamorphoses* printed by Daniel Bakkamude for the widow of Abraham de Wees, Amsterdam, 1671. The italic used in that book is the one which belongs to the roman in the specimen.

According to Van Krimpen this roman was cut by the same hand as the *Text Cursijf* (Great Primer italic)—also shewn in the Elsevier specimen—punches and matrices of which survive in the Enschedé Typefoundry at Haarlem. (Van Krimpen's *Romanée* roman was designed to match this italic.) The English-bodied roman and the Great Primer italic are shewn as *Kleine Augustyn Romein* and *Kleine Text Curcyf No. 2* in Johannes Enschedé's specimen-book of 1768, but Enschedé did not add—as he did in other instances—that the faces were cut by Christoffel van Dyck.

Jan van Krimpen's share in the production of Monotype 'Van Dijck' was 'chiefly advisory', as John Dreyfus remarks (in Van Krimpen's opinion 'fortunately', because he was strongly opposed to the copying and adapting of historical typefaces). Whatever he did for this series he did 'with love and application', yet in the end he was 'more opposed to it' than ever before, and he called the roman 'a doctored adaptation of a seventeenth-century Dutch face'. Monotype 'Van Dijck' nevertheless merits inclusion among the historical faces brought out by the Corporation. It was used at Cambridge in 1954 to compose an issue of *The Monotype Recorder* which described the work of Will Carter at the Rampant Lions Press. Van Krimpen presented to Cambridge six matrices struck from trial punches which were cut by hand in the Enschedé foundry under his direction; and Rowley Atterbury presented ten punches for a series of Van Dijck numerals which he had commissioned for his Westerham Press from Matthew Carter.

Who was Christoffel van Dyck and how did his punches and matrices come into the possession of Enschedé? Although he seems to have been a well-known punchcutter in his day and for many years afterwards, not much is known about him. Some information can be obtained from the application for the banns of his marriage in Amsterdam with Swaentje Harmens, widow of Joh. de Praet, on 11 October 1642. He was born at Dexheim (near Oppenheim in the Rhine Palatinate) in 1606 or 1607, for his age is given as 36 years; he had not been married before; he was living in the Breestraat, and he was typefounder by profession. Every now and then a trace of him is to be found in deeds. In 1642 he is mentioned as a goldsmith, living in the Breestraat. Some years later his address was on the Bloemgracht, and afterwards he moved to the Elandstraat. From a deed dated 27 November 1658 it can be concluded that he was also a punchcutter, for it was agreed that he should deliver punches and matrices for two sizes of Armenian type. He was buried on 23 November 1669 in Amsterdam.

His son Abraham, also a punchcutter and typefounder, carried on his father's business in the Elandstraat; not for long, however, because he died a few years later, at the end of February 1672. An advertisement in the *Oprechte Haarlemse*

Courant of 6 April 1673 announced that on Monday 10 April punches and matrices, together with the typefounder's requisites, would be put up for auction in the Elandstraat. No doubt, this was Van Dyck's typefoundry.

Daniel Elsevier, bookseller and printer at Amsterdam, bought the material. He used it for his own purposes and did not cast type for others. After his death in October 1680 his widow intended to sell the typefoundry and issued a specimen announcing the sale. The auction took place on 14 May 1681. In the heading of this specimen the faces are described as 'cut by the late Christoffel van Dyck', although some of them definitely came from other sources.

So far no evidence has been found to prove which faces were cut by Christoffel van Dyck. Dr Charles Enschedé suggested that only faces for which punches were sold in 1755 and 1767 were cut by Christoffel. Of the types mentioned above, punches were extant for the capitals of the *Text* roman only, not for the lower case; for the *Text* italic; and for the *Augustijn* roman and italic. Everybody seems to take it for granted that Van Dyck means Christoffel, but, after all, his son Abraham was a punch-cutter in his own right. The punches of the faces Abraham may have cut were of course included in the stock of the foundry. There is an obvious difference between *Text* and *Augustijn* italic: the first shows the hand of the artist, the second that of the faithful artisan. So it may very well be that the *Augustijn* italic was not cut by Christoffel but by his son Abraham. There is no way to tell whether they were cut by the same hand that cut *Text* italic, as no punches for the *Augustijn* survive.

Joseph Athias, a well-known Jewish printer in Amsterdam, bought the typefoundry at the sale in 1681. In June 1683 he advertised that the famous typefoundry of the late Christoffel van Dyck had again come into operation. A specimen is known to have been issued from Athias's address in the Swanenburg-straat. In 1686 the typefoundry was on the Nieuwe Heeren-

8-2

gracht opposite the Plantage, the address of the new plant to which the widow of Jan Jacobsz Schipper and Joseph Athias, associates in the printing and trading of English bibles, had moved the printing presses and the typefoundry. Soon afterwards financial troubles forced Athias to sell a half-share in the typefoundry to the Widow Schipper. Athias died in 1700 and his son Emanuel continued his father's business. A few years later he sold the other half-share in the typefoundry to Cornelia Cleyburg, *née* Schipper, formerly the widow of Pieter Dommer. The material descending from the typefoundry of Christoffel van Dyck was now owned by descendants of the Widow Schipper. It remained the property of members of the family until 1755 when it was again put up for auction.

Jan Roman, a bookseller in the Kalverstraat in Amsterdam, bought the typefoundry and advertised on 27 May 1755 that it was in operation. He issued a specimen which, except for the heading and a few additions, was printed from the same forme of type as the specimens of the Widow Elsevier and Joseph Athias. However, Roman decided to dispose of the typefoundry, and at the sale on 19 October 1767 the material was bought by the Brothers Ploos van Amstel, typefounders at Amsterdam, and Johannes Enschedé, typefounder at Haarlem. By mutual agreement they divided the punches and the matrices of the various faces. Thus Enschedé acquired among other lots the punches and the matrices for the faces on Great Primer and one on English body, roman as well as italic.

When Joh. Enschedé en Zonen acquired the typefoundry of Ploos van Amstel in 1799, Van Dyck's original material was brought together again, but the majority of the punches and the matrices was sold for the price of old metal in the nineteenth century, the faces then having lost their commercial value. Now that Van Dyck's designs have returned to favour, the small remainder of his handiwork is properly treasured.

NETTY HOEFLAKE

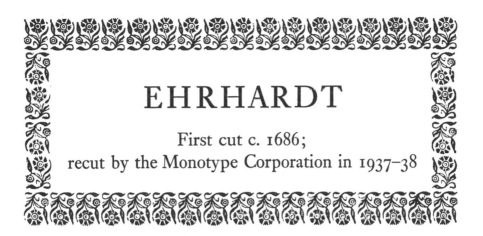

EHRHARDT

First cut c. 1686;
recut by the Monotype Corporation in 1937–38

The name means that this typeface is associated with the 'Holländische Schriften' that the Ehrhardt foundry in Leipzig showed in a specimen issued early in the eighteenth century. D. B. Updike reproduced part of it in his *Printing Types*, first published in 1922 (II, 43, 45). They are a range of romans and italics of stout Dutch character, some of which can be found in use as early as 1691 and several of which are in an Amsterdam typefounder's specimen issued between 1681 and 1717. A set of matrices for these types descended from Ehrhardt to the firm of Drugulin in Leipzig, which sold them in 1919 to the Stempel Typefoundry of Frankfurt am Main, from whom cast founts can be had.

In Germany these types of unknown origin are called 'Janson' after a little-known Leipzig typefounder who, it was supposed, might have cut them late in the seventeenth century. George Buday and I have given reasons for thinking that they were cut by Nicolas Kis, a Hungarian who was in Amsterdam working as a cutter of punches for type in 1680–9 and left a set of his matrices at Leipzig on his way home to Transylvania. Our article, printed in *The Linotype Matrix* no. 18 in 1954, convinced Stanley Morison that Kis was the author of Ehrhardt's 'Holländische Schriften'.

The letters of Monotype Ehrhardt are like those of the Janson, but the appearance of a page set in it is different. The Janson is more rotund and has greater contrast of thick and thin. It exemplifies the qualities that Joseph Moxon so admired in the 'late made Dutch Letters' when he wrote in 1683, 'the commodious Fatness they have beyond other Letters,...As also the true placing their Fats and their Leans, with the sweet driving them into one another'. In 'Ehrhardt' these qualities have been to some extent sacrificed to economy of space: it belongs to a late phase in Morison's thinking where he was less interested in the reproduction of an old type than in the production of one that gave good value in legibility.

The Monotype Corporation must often have considered adding a Janson series to its repertory. In Germany the original was famous for its use by the best printers, notably Drugulin for *Pan*, the luxurious periodical of art-criticism. D. B. Updike imported founts of it to America about 1914. Morison put a complete specimen of Stempel's Janson in his book *On Type Faces* in 1923. The Nonesuch Press had a case or two of the 14-point (Didot) in its cellar and set a few small books in it from 1927 onwards. Some of the Nonesuch fount eventually found its way to Cambridge:

ABCDEFGHIJKLMNOPQRSTUVWXYZ

ABCDEFGHIJKLMNOPQRSTUVWXYZ

abcdefghijklmnopqrstuvwxyz

abcdefghijklmnopqrstuvwxyz

The type was favoured enough to make the American Linotype and Monotype companies cut it for their machines. Mergenthaler Linotype had cut five sizes, 8 to 14-point, in

1933 and Lanston Monotype cut the 8-point in 1935. Both completed their series in 1937.

So it is not surprising that the Monotype Corporation made experimental letters for a 12-point (Didot) Janson at the request of the Haag-Drugulin printing house at Leipzig in April 1936. Morison stopped further work on the face; possibly he did not like following closely in the wake of other composing-machine makers; more likely he saw Janson as material, not for exact reproduction, but for treatment more to his mind. In January 1937 experimental work was begun on series 453, Ehrhardt.

It was another name for the same original model, but the change betokened a different treatment. The works at Salfords were instructed to make the Ehrhardt as big for its body as Imprint and in weight intermediate between that and Plantin. The name given to the new series is reason enough for supposing that the draughtsman was expected to render the 'Holländische Schriften' so far as the over-riding instructions for x-height and weight allowed. He made a very successful type of it. Morison thought the spacing between letters was too wide, and it was reduced.

Printers and publishers thirsting for novelty hurried the production. The Nonesuch Press wanted the 11-point, Bruce Rogers the 10-point, *Penrose Annual* urgently needed the 12-point. These sizes were generally available by the end of the year 1938. The Curwen Press requested an 8-point in 1943, but in wartime there were difficulties; the matrices were not delivered until early 1945. The 6-point was made in 1950, and big sizes, 24, 30, 36 and 72-point two years later.

Announcing the new series in *The Monotype Recorder* for 1938, a writer with the accents of Morison has this to say:

This article is set in 'Monotype' Ehrhardt, Series 453. Types in the manner made famous by Fleischman seem to have originated in Germany at the end of the seventeenth century. Several interesting founts were issued by the Leipzig and Frankfurt foundries between 1710 and the middle of the century.

Their novelty and merit lie in a certain modernity and liveliness of cut, relieved by a pleasing degree of condensation, which gives increased legibility by its generous x-height and, at the same time, conserves space.

It was an exercise in making a Fleischman out of a Kis, turning the humane and literate schoolmaster from Kolozsvár into the accurate drudge from Nuremberg. Fortunately, it was not carried very far.

Printers will always fall for a condensed type—but how often do we see Ehrhardt set solid? Save space one way and you must spend it the other. Morison (presumably, for he was advertiser as well as rationalist) wrote in the same *Recorder* about Times Wide type: 'The imperceptible condensation of Monotype Times New Roman puts it in a class by itself as a news face. In the wider book measures, however, condensation is no asset.'

On the need to save space by skilful type-design Morison in his later years wrote more than once. In his article on 'Leipzig as a Centre of Typefounding' (*Signature* XI, 1939) he says:

But the justification for printing is not primarily stylistic; first and foremost its justification is economic. It follows, therefore, that appreciation of the art of lettering as applied by punch-cutters to the service of the printing trade must reckon with the element of economy. Indeed it seems to the present writer not too much to say, regarding book-typography in the period after Garamond and Granjon, that it is in the exploitation of the available space, rather than in conspicuous details such as serifs and stresses, there lies the secret of successful type-design.

He puts it succinctly in his essay 'On the Classification of Typographical Variations' (1963): 'type-design consciously viewed as a means of reducing the real space occupied by the letters while maintaining their apparent size'.

These extracts provide a context for the instructions given for the drawing of Ehrhardt.

It is a successful type-face. I think Kis would have liked this series. He would certainly have liked the regularity and smooth finish given to it by the industrialized process. The grace of his alphabets is not wholly lost by any means. He wrote in his *Mentség* (Apology for his life) that the master who taught him his trade could not cut italics and made Kis cut them for him. The Janson italic is excellent, and the Ehrhardt italic has withstood a degree of condensation fairly well.

Morison did not know, and could not have known until George Buday translated the relevant passages in the *Mentség* into a western-European language, that Kis cut a second range of roman and italic types, bigger on the body, more condensed, and more modern in fashion than the Janson. Updike, with his wonderful eye for the significant, chose half a page set in some of them to reproduce in *Printing Types* (i, 171). They were made for the Grand-Ducal Press at Florence, then tenanted by G. F. Cecchi. Kis wrote that the Grand Duke sent emissaries round Europe to find the best letter-cutter and they spent a month trying to persuade him to take charge of a typefoundry in Florence. He was more interested in printing the Bible in Hungarian with what he considered the best type and the emendations to the grammar and spelling that he favoured.

His second thoughts in type are very much like the Ehrhardt, though paler. To have taken this Tuscan type for a model would have avoided some infelicities in the shapes of the capitals that are a little troublesome in the Janson and Ehrhardt.

HARRY CARTER

ROMULUS

DESIGNED BY JAN VAN KRIMPEN

JOINTLY PRODUCED IN 1931–39
BY ENSCHEDÉ EN ZONEN
AND THE MONOTYPE CORPORATION

Display sizes of Romulus were acquired by the Press in 1948 for use in ceremonial printing for the Royal Society, and for a variety of elegant jobbing work commissioned by other customers. Romulus was designed by Jan van Krimpen (1892–1957), an eminent Dutch typographer, type designer (and occasionally stamp designer) employed by the ancient printing house and typefoundry of Enschedé en Zonen in Haarlem. Their most skilled hand punchcutter, P. H. Raedisch, interpreted the original drawings and cut trial founts under Van Krimpen's close supervision.

Van Krimpen's gift for type design was greatly admired by Morison, who had praised the Dutchman's first type (Lutetia, 1925) as being 'a new type, underived from any historic predecessor or school'. He found it exceedingly handsome, wrote to compliment its designer, and later arranged for Lutetia to be cut by the Monotype Corporation. From the late twenties the two men met frequently and spanned the intervals with an ardent correspondence. Van Krimpen was a keen reader of all that Morison wrote, and was particularly impressed by his essay in *The Fleuron* v entitled 'Towards an Ideal Italic'. It argued that the only function of a secondary (italic) type was to support the body letter (roman). This it could only do if it possessed sufficient differential indications; but since harmony between the two forms could only be obtained by conservation of similarity, differentia in the secondary type were to be kept to a minimum. After dismissing secondary forms of different size, weight or colour, Morison concluded that the only good alternative was 'a sloped type, sufficiently inclined to be differentiated from the primary type, yet following its design as closely as possible'. The secondary letter was therefore obliged to agree in all essentials of design with the text type, and to be free of informal or cursive characteristics. The perfect italic was to be a slanted roman. And this was precisely what Van Krimpen provided for Romulus.

To draw a slanted roman was a fairly simple matter for Van Krimpen. But difficulties arose in cutting the type; several roman letters developed awkward overhangs when slanted at an italic angle, thereby causing trouble in making them fit together evenly. But the greatest difficulty of all arose in the eye of the beholder. In a review of Romulus in *Signature* XIII (1940), an observant scholar of printing types, A. F. Johnson, commented that sloped roman 'may be logical but results in a stiff and monotonous letter'. Morison later told Harry Carter that the objection to sloped roman was that the average reader did not notice that it was sloped, and he admitted that the italic he designed for Times New Roman 'owed more to Didot than to dogma'.

Romulus was intended to form part of an extensive family of related types, with various weights and widths of roman and sloped roman, four sans-serifs and a Greek. In addition the designer included a *cancelleresca bastarda*, an elegant type so rich in cursive qualities that the adoption of a sloped roman was made to seem of slight importance. Only the roman, sloped roman and semibold were made by the Monotype Corporation, and this range only came on the market at the outbreak of war. Morison considered the sloped roman an impediment in text composition, but after the war he approved the purchase of a range of Romulus in display sizes. These had been studied with close attention and increasing admiration by the writer of this note, then an Assistant University Printer, when he compiled for the designer's sixtieth birthday a record, *The Work of Jan van Krimpen*, (London, 1952) for which Morison wrote an important foreword. Any reader whose curiosity about the entire Romulus 'family' remains unsatisfied will find on pp. 36–46 of that book a full showing and description of what it comprised.

JOHN DREYFUS

NOTES

(For contributions to the following notes special thanks are due to Harry Carter, Nicolas Barker and John Dreyfus.)

18 Morison wrote a memoir of Reed which appeared in the Cambridge University Printer's series of presentation books (Stanley Morison: *Talbot Baines Reed, Author, Bibliographer, Typefounder*; Cambridge, 1960).

21 (line 6) Rogers' report was reproduced in the same series (*Report on the Typography of the Cambridge University Press prepared in 1917 at the request of the Syndics*; Cambridge, 1950). Another edition was printed for the Wynkyn de Worde Society in 1968.

   (line 22) According to Mason's notebooks (quoted in *Monotype Newsletter* 71) the type on which Imprint was based was Caslon's Great Primer. Dibdin's approval of the type referred to by Morison has not been traced.

22 See Typographica Plantiniana, II: 'Early Inventories of Punches, Matrices and Moulds in the Plantin-Moretus Archives', *De Gulden Passer*, 38, p. 42; Antwerp, 1960.

28 Richard Austin was the subject of a study by Morison issued in the Cambridge University Printer's series of presentation books (*Richard Austin, Engraver to the Printing Trade between the years 1788 and 1830*; Cambridge, 1937).

34 Although Morison may have been justified in his criticism of Pierpont's attitude, the latter had in fact many accomplishments to his credit, notably in the development of the Typograph machine and the raising of the Monotype works at Horley to a high state of efficiency, especially in the matrix-making department. [J.G.D.]

49 In his edition of Pietro Bembo's *De Aetna*, published in 1969,

Giovanni Mardersteig included an essay on the types in which the book was printed. He recounted how in 1930 he had told Stanley Morison of his plan to have an old type-face recut by the French punchcutter Charles Malin, and how Morison had persuaded him to take Griffo's as a model. The outcome was a type which Mardersteig entitled 'Griffo' and which he justly claimed was closer to the original and retained more of its elegance than did the Monotype face, but without being an exact copy. Indeed, this would have been impracticable, owing to Griffo's use of numerous variations of the more frequent letters, designed in Mardersteig's view to avoid monotony and so cause the printed book to compare favourably with the manuscripts still preferred by the *cognoscenti*.

51 Mr Fairbank has suggested that this sentence implies that he had specifically been commissioned to design an italic in the manner of the chancery cursive to be used in association with a particular roman, which was not, in fact, true. He has also stated that changes were made to some lower-case letters which he regretted (*Journal of the Society for Italic Handwriting*, No. 33).

57 (line 12)   Emery Walker's name should be added to those of Bridges, Johnston and Fairbank.
(line 27)   The earliest cursive Brief is, in fact, not earlier than Nicolas V (1447–55). [N.B.]

59 (line 14)   The idea came to Johnston and Kessler from Emery Walker in 1911. His model was Tagliente's design. Johnston began working on it in 1912. See John Dreyfus, *Italic Quartet*; Cambridge, 1966.
(line 26)   In fact, Morison did not model his script on fig. 180 in Johnston's book until the early 1920s. From 1913 until then he used an upright hand, very small, not unlike Johnston's own. [N.B.]

60 For *Giovo* read *Giovio*.

64   The 'Caractères de l'Université' were roman and italic for three bodies, *gros canon, petit canon* and *gros parangon*, for which 'Nicolas Jannon' sold matrices to Sébastien Cramoisy, Directeur de l'Imprimerie Royale, in 1641 (*L'Art du livre à l'Imprimerie Nationale*, p. 56; Paris, 1951). Nicolas Jannon is otherwise not known; it is probably a mistake for Jean, the printer and typefounder of Sedan. He worked for the Protestant academy there; hence a likely reason for the name given to the types. Jannon's italics for *petit canon* and *gros parangon* are shown in a specimen of the types of the Imprimerie Royale of 1643 (J. Veyrin-Forrer and A. Jammes, *Les Premiers caractères de l'Imprimerie Royale*, Documents typographiques français, II; Paris, 1958). Smaller faces, reproducing Jannon's design, appear to have been made by order of Arthur Christian in time for the Paris Exposition of 1900 (Paul Beaujon, 'The Garamond Types', *The Fleuron* v, 170). There is no reason to think that Jannon tried to copy Garamond's types. His design is original and characteristic of the seventeenth century insofar as he increased the x-height. The only significant dates that are known for Garamond's career are those of his cutting the 'Grecs du Roi' (1541–6), his venture into publishing (1545) and his death (1561). Morison quotes or deduces dates from a document written or dictated by Guillaume II Le Bé in 1643, which Miss O. F. Abbott, researching for Morison, discovered in private hands. It has since been published— *Sixteenth-Century French Typefounders: the Le Bé Memorandum*, Documents typographiques français, III; Paris, 1967. That is the only authority for Garamond's being apprenticed to Augereau and working for Haultin and in Chevallon's house. The document contains many inaccuracies and should be treated with reserve. The belief that Garamond learned from Tory rests on slight grounds (Beaujon, *op. cit.* p. 133). Jeanne Veyrin-Forrer, in her monograph on Augereau, con-

cludes that it is 'très probable' that he played some part in producing type for De Colines ('Antoine Augereau, graveur de lettres et imprimeur parisien, vers 1485–1534', *Paris et Île de France, Mémoires*, VIII, pp. 112–13; Paris, 1957). The article by Beaujon owed a good deal to one by Jean Paillard, *Claude Garamond, Étude historique*, published in 1914 by the Parisian typefounder Ollière. Paillard was the first to challenge the attribution of the Caractères de l'Université to Garamond. His essay has not been given the recognition that it deserved. There is no justification for the statement that De Colines, Tory and Estienne were using type of a new fashion by 1528. Estienne had type of the Aldine design by 1530 and De Colines by 1531. De Colines printed for Tory with his new type in 1531–2 (A. F. Johnson, 'Geofroy Tory', *The Fleuron* VI, p. 64). [H.C.]

65 (line 9) The memorandum by Guillaume II Le Bé is the authority for Garamond's working for Haultin (a thing hard to reconcile with the dates of contemporary references to Haultin). Le Bé goes on to say that, having done so, Garamond began work on his own account in the house of Chevallon. For André read Claude. Later in life Garamond cut a fine italic for *Gros Romain* (Great Primer) body. The design is typically 'Old Face', i.e. a blend of the Aldine and the Roman Chancery styles, and the type is, perhaps, the first of that kind. (Reproduction in H. Carter, *A View of Early Typography*; Oxford, 1969, fig. 83.) [H.C.]

(line 34) Janot must be Denys Janot, Imprimeur du Roi pour la langue française. His italic in *Le Theatre des bons engins*, 1539 (?), is reproduced in Morison's *Four Centuries of Fine Printing* (1949 ed., p. 145). [H.C.]

66 For *the spirit rather of Paris than of Geneva, whence Jannon came* read *the spirit of Geneva, whence Jannon came, rather than of Paris*. This alteration was agreed by Morison in correspondence with Van Krimpen (4–10 May 1957) and the

sentence as worded above was quoted by Van Krimpen in his article 'On Related Type Faces' in *Book Design and Production*, I (London 1958), p. 28. He added a footnote: 'I have here, with Mr Morison's consent, changed the text of the original so as to make it read as he intended it to do'. [J.G.D.]

69 This was his prefatory note to Chambellan's *Pia et Religiosa Meditatio*.

70 According to Harry Carter the need to mate roman and italic was first recognized by François Guyot in the 1540's (*A View of Early Typography*, Oxford, 1969).

71 (line 7) A typical bold face roman, called '*gros canon des missels*', is offered as an alternative to the normal in *Epreuves des caractères du fond des Sanlecques* (Paris, 1757). It was probably cut early in the seventeenth century. [H.C.]
(line 21) Three greeks and two or three italics by Granjon were among the faces for which Fell bought matrices in 1672. The matrices were ceded to the University by Fell's executors in 1690. See Morison's *John Fell, the University Press, and the 'Fell' Types* (Oxford, 1967), pp. 139–42. The Long Primer italic is probably his. [H.C.]

72 Granjon cut exotic typefaces, Armenian, Syriac, Cyrillic, and Arabic, commissioned by Gregory XIII in 1578–83, before he began work for the Medici Press (II. D. L. Vervliet, 'Robert Granjon à Rome, 1578–1589', *Bulletin de l'Institut historique belge à Rome*, XXXVIII, 1967, 177–231). [H.C.]

73 Anyone who looks at the reproduction of the specimen of the Imprimerie Royale of 1643 (see the note to p. 64 above) will find it hard to believe that the italic of Monotype Series 156 renders the design of Granjon's gros canon and not that of Jannon's *petit canon* or *gros parangon*. It has evident features of Jannon's style, the wide *A*, the serifs of

his *R*, the multiplicity of extravagantly swash letters, besides the generally cramped look instead of the ease and fluency of Granjon. There must have been some confusion in Morison's mind when he wrote this. (He has also slipped up in giving the date 1530 in the heading of this section on p. 67. It has never been claimed that Granjon was active before 1543 at the earliest. Even in Morison's own *John Fell* there is nothing to substantiate a date as early as 1530.) The Le Bé inventory copied in 1730 has been published with an introduction and notes by Morison and André Jammes (*L'Inventaire de la fonderie Le Bé.* Documents typographiques français, 1; Paris, 1957). [H.C.]

77 The facts have now been sorted out by James Mosley in his facsimile of P. S. Fournier's *Modéles des Caractères* (London, 1965).

80 Barbou has now been cut in five additional sizes from 8 to 12-point.

82 No Caslon specimen book of 1808 is known to exist, although there were some broadsides of that date. The next issue of a specimen book was in 1816. [N.B.]

88 The serifs of Bodoni's 1788 design were as sharp, if not sharper, but they were not bracketed. [N.B.]

90 According to Rogers, 'there were only two cases of each size and I bought the English size and set a few sample pages of Virgil's *Georgics.* Mr Mifflin saw them at an exhibition and wanted to know why they were not used. After some consideration I sold them back to Riverside and we began setting the *Rubaiyat* in it. Although it was the first of the Riverside Press editions the Michaelangelo *Sonnets* came out in advance of it, as we had only enough type to set four pages at a time, electrotype, distribute and then set the next four. It took about a year...The Pica size was used in four little books by Leon H. Vincent published in 1900 *et seq.*' (Letter to John Carter, 15 January 1954.)

96 The reference here is to Raffaello Bertieri, *Il Caratteri Umanistico di Antonio Sinibaldi.* [N.B.]

101 The Perpetua punches which Malin engraved were acquired by Ernest Ingham, who later presented them to the Cambridge University Press.

105 It is doubtful whether Morison's account of his liaison with Lardent is correct. More probably, Morison provided Lardent with a specimen of 'Plantin' type (see plate 10*a* of Nicolas Barker's biography), accompanied by written or oral instructions, and Lardent produced outline drawings on which Morison indicated the alterations he wished to be made. This would conform with Lardent's own statement quoted by James Moran (*Stanley Morison: his Typographic Achievement*, pp. 127–8) and with the recollections of Mr A. Campbell, a colleague of Lardent.

109 A weakness of The Times type was the thinness of the walls of the Linotype matrices, which led to frequent replacements. Furthermore, it had been designed for printing on high-quality newsprint and at comparatively low speed— advantages it was necessary to forgo for the sake of economy in the post-war years. A new type, 'Times-Europa', designed by Walter Tracy, was substituted in 1972.

INDEX